Sunrise to Paradise

The Story of
Mount Rainier National Park

Ruth Kirk

UNIVERSITY OF WASHINGTON PRESS

Seattle and London

This book has been published with the cooperative support of
The Washington State History Museum, KCTS Television, and
The Mount Rainier, North Cascades & Olympic Fund, to celebrate
the centennial of the establishment of Mount Rainier National Park.

Copyright @ 1999 by the
University of Washington Press
Printed in Hong Kong

Library of Congress Cataloging in Publication Data
Kirk, Ruth
    Sunrise to paradise: the story of Mount Rainier
National Park / Ruth Kirk.
        p.   cm.
    Includes bibliographical references and index.
    ISBN 0–295–97770–1 (cloth: alk. paper).—
ISBN 0–295–97771–X (paper: alk. paper)
    1. Mount Rainier National Park (Wash.)—History.
I. Title
F897.R2K53   1999
979.7'782—dc21   98–43072
                                                       CIP

Contents

Foreword

I live where I do because of Mount Rainier. In this regard, my family and I are hardly unique. My wife and I selected our homesite on Tumwater Hill (in the Olympia area) twenty-five years ago because of the spectacular vista offered by the Mountain every day it is "out." One of my favorite pastimes is to follow the grand seasonal arc of sunrises from the southeast horizon in the dead of winter to the northeast in summer; Mount Rainier is always framed by this heavenly semicircle. This custom of mine, like those of many others, is rooted in the perception of the mountain's immutability.

The people in our neighborhood think we have the best view of Mount Rainier to be found anywhere—although no doubt there are partisans of other favored vantage points. We all prize the immediacy and sense of connection to the landscape that the mountain provides, perhaps in ways that are not fully conscious to us. These physical, emotional, psychological relationships with Mount Rainier, all of them ultimately personal, are the underpinning of Ruth Kirk's *Sunrise to Paradise: The Story of Mount Rainier National Park*.

I am honored to write these few words about and for the Mountain and the book. This publication of the University of Washington Press is the companion to an exhibit by the same title at the Washington State History Museum in Tacoma, which I direct, and a television documentary produced by KCTS-9 in Seattle. The Mountain has brought our three institutions together in an interpretive partnership to observe the Mount Rainier National Park centennial and to salute the coming century of the Mountain. It has provided both a common ground and a visual focus for us as organizations, just as the Mountain does more generally for the people of Washington today and as it has done for generations of people before the State of Washington existed. Rainier has been widely appropriated as an icon by our culture, but we are only now, with this celebratory investigation, analyzing why this is so. Ruth Kirk, in the stories she tells, addresses the question with great suggestive insight.

Mount Rainier is truly a Wonderland in the Sky. It is our Shangri-La. But it is also very much a landscape at risk from overuse, urban pollution and, in a way, from itself, given its fundamental volcanic identity. Though the Mountain is more than the park, it is nonetheless true that the national park status is the system modern society has

(Above) Paradise snow play; (opposite page) Christine Falls

put in place as a stewardship device. This park, our nation's fifth national park, is one of Washington's principal environmental and economic assets. We treasure it. A number of western states, even in quite recent times, have resisted the creation of federal stewardship entities such as national parks. But Mount Rainier National Park is and has always been a natural fit to our view of ourselves and the world.

Mount Rainier is the predominant emblem of Washington, with its image being carried far and wide on our state license plates. But the visual and mythic power of the Mountain has captivated people for a longer time and from farther away than many of us might realize. My good friend Allen Pinkham, the former Nez Perce Tribal Executive Committee Chairman, says that the tribe once had a runner who, before white people arrived, would cover vast distances in just a few days. He made many trips to see the western people and eventually he became known as "Tahoma," which is the Puyallup tribe's name for the Mountain. Tahoma, the Nez Perce runner, bore the Mountain's mark.

In various ways, the mark of the Mountain is on us all.

David L. Nicandri
Director, Washington State Historical Society

Backcountry patrol cabin, Indian Henry's Hunting Ground

Preface

I want this to be a something-for-everybody book, even though I know the goal is unrealistic. One set of pages cannot please all of Mount Rainier's varied aficionados. My decision has been to sample the many splendors and stories of the Mountain, not to attempt an all-inclusive report. And I have tended to emphasize the early years, highlighting events and persons that set the pattern of the park we know today.

Rainier is unique: it is a wilderness that enhances city views. In its beginning days as a national park, urban folks helped to steer policy, and they continue to do so one hundred years later. People feel proprietary about Rainier, whether they set their boots—and wheels—on the Mountain's slopes or admire its summit from afar but have no desire to enter the park's gate. No other national park has such a large, close-by, vocal, devoted constituency. In the 1890s, worries about campers' carelessness at Paradise and the poaching of wildlife contributed to citizen support for congressional action to establish the park. In the 1990s, public input is helping to shape the park's management plan for the coming decades.

When the park was halfway to its centennial year, my ranger husband Louis and I moved into the log house at Nisqually Entrance with our two young sons. We had transferred from stations in Death Valley, California, and Organ Pipe Cactus, on Arizona's border with Mexico, and the driver who brought our furniture commented: "You've moved from the ridiculous to the sublime. You've found Paradise." For three weeks we neither saw the Mountain nor knew precisely where to look for it. Then came the morning when the clouds lifted and the peak stood clear, white, and huge—the sort of mountain that children instinctively draw. We knew the driver was right.

Mount Rainier is the fifth highest peak in the United States outside of Alaska, and it soars higher above its immediate base than does any other in the forty-eight contiguous states. (The second highest is Telescope Peak's rise above the desolate, below-sea-level floor of Death Valley.) Part of Rainier's appeal is this lone rise: no other peaks shoulder it. Part of the appeal, too, centers in the raw power that built the volcano (and may tear it apart), and in the ceaseless grind of the glaciers that sheath it and shape it.

My memory of living at Rainier centers, in part, on the spectacle of the Mountain. We first climbed to the summit in a July blizzard. The second time, we climbed with the legendary Assistant Chief Ranger Bill Butler, carrying cement to the top so as to install a new benchmark. Surveyors had just remeasured Rainier and had added two feet to its official height, bringing it to 14,410 feet. We hiked trails, usually without meeting other hikers, and we skied unbroken midweek snow slopes while city folk were bound to city tasks. When a winter storm knocked out the park's power, our boys built an igloo and offered it for safe storage of our refrigerator's contents.

My memory is also made up of small touches. We watched pioneer violets and calypso orchids bloom beyond our porch each spring, and we savored the purple and red and white of lupine and paintbrush and avalanche lilies in the high summer meadows. We cherished dappled fawns and a lone bear cub, awoke to the disputes of raccoons and spotted skunks sharing quarters under the house, and were misled by the odd squeaking of bats in the wall at the head of our bed. My husband thought it was I snoring. I thought it was he.

Work on this book has triggered happy nostalgia and an impression that the 1950s were perhaps the best of all times for living at Rainier. Formalities and paperwork were minimal. One spring my husband and another ranger built a cabin from scrounged materials—without plans or permission—because they wanted to get the summer-season ranger family at Nisqually out of the unending dampness of living in a tent and into the warmth of a cabin. A do-it spirit characterized ranger life (and, after its many years as living quarters, that same cabin has been dragged up the hill and tacked onto one of the houses at Nisqually as an external storeroom). Sometimes the do-it spirit ultimately proved unwise. For example: Wind-toppled trees along Tahoma Creek were commercially salvaged in the 1950s, and the superintendent told the two Nisqually rangers to turn the cleared area into a campground. In the 1960s the campground became a picnic area, but then the site had to be closed. Outburst floods, a hallmark of glacierized volcanoes, repeatedly swept through the area. Such hazards seemed theoretical in our day. Now we know that they are awesomely real. The danger of floods and mudflows are a major consideration when planning for the Tahoma Creek area as well as for the entire park.

I recall fondly the energy and innocence of our day without commending all of its practices. For the sake of safeguarding yesterday's cultural landscapes, I applaud the

The Mountain from Stevens Canyon, early fall

National Historic District status that keeps Nisqually Entrance, and the rest of the park's human-built environment, as-is rather than permitting further additions such as the Nisqually cabin. For today's stewardship of tomorrow's park, I rejoice that Rainier's ecosystem is cared for by a dozen staff management scientists, many with PhDs, who work with non-staff research scientists in other government agencies and at the University of Washington. In our day, a single naturalist tried to become knowledgeable about the park's geology, biology, and history, and to convey all of this information to park administrators, hikers, campers, and motorists. Before our day—in the late 1920s—the National Park Service had no internal program of biological study. The situation so distressed George M. Wright, assistant naturalist at Yosemite, that his do-it spirit, plus independent wealth, led him to finance personally the beginnings of national park biology and public education programs. (The Seattle Mountaineers built a monument to Wright's memory at Mount Rainier. Only the plaque survives today.)

Wright and his mentor Joseph Grinnell, head of the University of California's Museum of Vertebrate Zoology, together with zoologist Tracy Storer, wrote that studying biology in national parks made them increasingly aware that species in the wild have developed "a finely adjusted interrelation . . . amounting to a mutual interdependence." They noted, with foresight, that stewardship of the natural processes in parks would forever be complicated by the presence of large numbers of people. Park visitors were a factor that "never existed before" and might cause a "very wide range of maladjustments."

Automobiles were revolutionizing park patterns in the early 1900s by bringing people to the Mountain; now they send exhaust fumes. The Puget Sound megalopolis sprawls upwind only fifty to seventy miles distant, and its motor vehicles are the number-one polluters of the Mountain's air. The coal-burning Centralia Power Plant, thirty miles upwind, ranks second as an offender; it has caused a full third of the park's sulphur dioxide pollution. In the case of the power plant, however, a solution has emerged: namely, a long, patient series of CDM sessions (Collaborative Decision Making). For nearly two years, businessmen, environmental overseers, land managers, and scientists have exchanged confidential data concerning everything from atmospheric particulate counts at Paradise, to the technology of smokestack scrubbers, to the socioeconomic reality of 700 jobs in Centralia that depend on the coal mine and the steam plant. Result? By 2002, scrubbers will eliminate ninety percent of the sulphur dioxide emitted at Centralia. A one-time exemption from taxes on buying and installing emission control equipment helps with this.

The cleaner emissions should lower the acid levels in park snowpacks and lakes and streams. Salamanders and frogs should be less threatened by changes in water chemistry, and the leaves of plants may be less subject to spotting and unknown damage because of changes in air chemistry. It would be an irony indeed if the burning of fossil fuels, which derive from plants, were to disrupt the heather communities on the high slopes of Rainier. For 10,000 years the heather has survived change. Maybe it would—or will—endure this newest change, maybe not.

No one knows. Nor can anyone yet fully sort out which particulates cause what problems. Pulp mills, aluminum plants, oil refineries, open-air burning, boats, lawnmowers, fireplaces, and wood stoves all contribute to polluting the park.

No book is the product solely of its author, and the statement is more true of this book than of any other in my experience. People at the park helped immeasurably— Bill Briggle, Donna Rahier, Craig Strong, Ted Stout, Gregg Sullivan, Barbara Samora, Regina Rochefort, Julie Hoser, Rich Lechleitner, Gary Ahlstrand, and Rhea Gillispie. Superintendent Bill Briggle even let me stay in the house next to one of our two old houses at Nisqually while I was researching and interviewing in the park.

Tribal members Bill Iyall and Karen Reed-Squally spoke with me of family traditions and contemporary Native Americans' regard for the Mountain they call *Tahoma*. Patrick Pringle, of the Washington Department of Natural Resources, and Carolyn Driedger, of the U.S. Geological Survey, generously provided information and read and corrected manuscript pages. Anne Heinitz, Department of Natural Resources, worked with Patrick Pringle to generate the book's shaded relief map, which is based on digital elevation data. Bob McIntyre, Jr., son of a former Mount Rainier National Park chief naturalist, guided me through the grandma's-attic collection of Rainier files at the federal archives in Seattle and willingly researched a myriad of points there and in other repositories, often doing so on short notice, always doing so with a cheerfulness that was immensely heartening.

Similarly, Nancy Shader, working at the archives to organize the park's photo files, repeatedly disrupted herself to rummage after choice images for this book. Richard Engeman and Carla Rickerson produced a wealth of photos from the Special Collections at Allen Library, University of Washington, as did Elaine Miller and Joy Werlink at the Washington State Historical Society's research center. Mark Lembersky generously offered access to his outstanding photographs of the Mountain as well as encouragement for the entire project. Denis S. Olson also provided photographs, and Rod Slemmons contributed expertise, patiently photographing artifacts belonging to the park and the Washington State Historical Society, and re-photographing historic pictures. Dee Molenaar painted geological views of the Mountain especially for the book.

Finally, let me deeply thank the authors of the sidebar commentaries included in these pages. Many are friends from shared Rainier years, persons who played important roles in the history of the Mountain. My thanks, too, to David Nicandri, director of the Washington State Historical Society, who effectively juggles more responsibilities and opportunities than any other one person I know, and who therefore said "yes" when asked to contribute a foreword for this book. And my thanks to many persons at the University of Washington Press, especially to Michael Duckworth, Gretchen Van Meter, and Bob Hutchins.

For the Mountain itself, my awe and fond good wishes for the second century as a national park. If love could shine through ink, these pages would glow.

Ruth Kirk

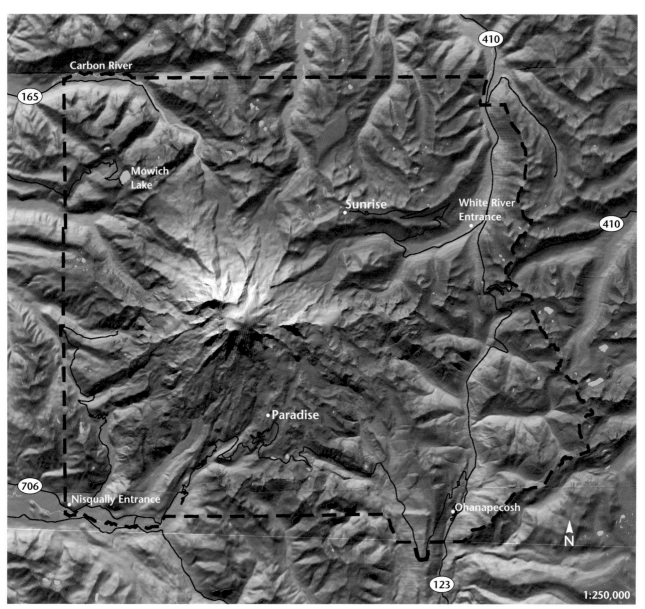

410

165

Carbon River

Mowich
Lake

Sunrise

White River
Entrance

410

706

Nisqually Entrance

•Paradise

Ohanapecosh

N

123

1:250,000

Shaded-relief, digital image of Mount Rainier National Park, computer-generated from topographic data
(Some roads are closed in winter or for other reasons; inquire.)

– – – Park Boundary
————— Road

Sunrise to Paradise

The Story of Mount Rainier National Park

PART I

The Mountain

Mention "the Mountain" anywhere from Everett to Olympia or in the Yakima Valley, and the reference is clear: only Rainier is "the Mountain." Other peaks need their names to identify them. Not Rainier.

Similarly, to say that "the Mountain is out" both announces the weather and declares affection for Washington's scenic monarch. Rain pounding down or vapor rising back up often merges horizon and sky into unified murk and hides the Mountain. But when the Mountain is out, drivers and walkers alter their routes to hold it in view as long as possible. And like birders adding to a life list, they exult in having glimpsed Rainier from some newly discovered vantage point.

"We had an epiphany on I-90 one below-freezing February morning," says Spokane history professor Robert Carriker. "We were in the middle of the state, driving across the endless fields west of Ritzville, and . . . whoa! There it was. The Mountain in all its grandeur. I mentally marked the spot, then reversed course by cutting across the median at the next place where a sign said not to. I wanted to take another run and be sure I wasn't seeing a mirage. No, I was correct the first time. It was real. It was Rainier.

"So I did some calculations and realized it isn't theoretically possible to see as far as we did (about 160 miles), not in today's pollution-filled environment. And I remembered that William Clark once peered out (October 19, 1805) about where McNary Dam is fastened to the Washington side of the Columbia River and he could see all the way to Mount Adams, though he mistook it for St. Helens. Ritzville to Rainier is a farther view, but still, Clark's experience shows I'm not the only person to have had such a vision. That made me feel kind of comfortable all the way to Ryegrass Pass, where cresting Vantage Hill we could confirm that 'Yup! That is the Mountain we saw.' What a drive we had that day."

Measuring the Mountain

Mount Rainier belongs as much to Washington's psychological landscape as to its physical topography. For some people, this translates into intimate acquaintance: an azure sky punctured close-up by a boldly gleaming white peak; the bloom of summer avalanche lilies and lupines chasing snowbanks uphill; the mysterious blue-white depths of a glacier's crevasse; marmots shrieking like divas and dropping into their burrows; new snow pillowed on tree branches. For other Washingtonians, the Mountain is best cherished from afar. It graces the distance. Leave it there.

As a corporate logo, Rainier serves candy makers, beer companies, apple growers, plumbing shops, and banks. As a civic logo, it graces tribal police emblems, municipal let-terheads, coffee mugs, and Washington state automobile license plates. Television viewers see the Mountain dubbed in as background for Puget Sound newscasters. Postage stamps carried it across the continent in 1934 to honor national parks, and in 1989 to celebrate the centennial of statehood. (A 1953 stamp marked the centennial of Washington's separation from Oregon into a territory of its own. It includes a peak that may or may not be *the* Mountain). In the early 1900s, railroad companies featured Rainier in their Northwest boosterism. In the 1930s and forties, so did See-America-Firsters.

Politicians have fanned the boosterism. In 1913 Representative Albert Johnson of Tacoma proposed construction of "Washington West" at Mount Tacoma (an alternative, much-debated name for Rainier). He claimed

Mark Glickman: A Rabbi's View

Raised in Chicago and educated in St. Louis, Jerusalem, and Cincinnati, Rabbi Glickman had no experience with mountains until he moved with his family to Tacoma, Washington, from Dayton, Ohio. He intends to climb Mount Rainier.

I will never forget the first time I saw Mount Rainier. It was in December of 1996 and I was in Tacoma to interview at Temple Beth El for the rabbinic post I currently hold. It was cloudy the day I arrived, and the next morning I groggily opened the window of the hotel room in downtown Tacoma where I was staying, and there it was! I did what I imagine almost all people do when they see the Mountain for the first time:

I gasped.

One of my few hesitations about moving to the Northwest is that my two small children will become so accustomed to seeing Mount Rainier that they will fail to gasp.

Soon after beginning to live here and seeing the Mountain regularly, I realized that Judaism gives words to the gasp so many of us utter when seeing spectacular, awesome sights of nature. We Jews are instructed to say a *brachah* on such occasions, a blessing praising God for having created a world that holds such majesty. Thus was born the Temple Beth El Mountain Brachah Society. To participate, members of our congregation were asked to say the Mountain Brachah upon first seeing Mount Rainier on days that it is "out." In return, they would get a membership card; they would be invited to a picnic at, or in view of, the Mountain in the spring; and they would receive an official Mountain

MEMBERSHIP CARD

THE TEMPLE BETH EL MOUNTAIN BRACHAH SOCIETY

בָּרוּךְ אַתָּה יהוה אֱלֹהֵינוּ מֶלֶךְ הָעוֹלָם,
עֹשֶׂה מַעֲשֵׂה בְרֵאשִׁית

BLESSED ARE YOU ADONAI OUR GOD
RULER OF THE UNIVERSE
WHO PERFORMS THE ACTS OF CREATION

Brachah Society T-shirt. We were hoping that 200 people in our little 330-family congregation would sign up for this project. But more than 400 people made the pledge.

Why has this struck such a chord? I am sure there are many reasons. For one, many of us are indeed thankful to live within sight of such a spectacular mountain. Even more than that, it seems to me many of us are starving for a sense of awe, an awareness that there is something bigger and more enduring than ourselves. Simply looking at Mount Rainier brings such awareness, and reciting the blessing that has been said by Jews for centuries adds powerfully to the impact.

I have lived in Tacoma for several months now, and I still gasp whenever I see the Mountain. I pray I never lose that. The Mountain looks different every time I see it: sometimes blue, sometimes pink, sometimes hiding among clouds. Like God, the Mountain is always there, even if obscured from view. It beckons me to climb it one day. I don't know if I have the stamina, but if I do, the real thrill will not be "conquering" the Mountain, for God's creations are not to be conquered. Rather the real thrill will be to stand atop Mount Rainier and look out to the four corners of the world, standing in awe before God's majestic creation.

FRESH TRACKS

Postage stamps, advertising posters, letterheads, candy boxes, beer trays, and the plastic bag of a Yakima Valley apple grower all feature Mount Rainier as logo.

For a few fleeting minutes at sunrise, Mount Rainier casts a perfect, triple-peaked shadow onto clouds, a rare occurrence.

The Mountain's sunset shadow stretches across the lowlands as an evanescent pyramid, first expanding, then vanishing.

This 1878 engraving is captioned: "New Tacoma and Mount Rainier, Washington Territory, terminus of the Northern Pacific Railroad. Altitude Mt. Rainier 14,440 feet." The railroad had reached Tacoma in 1873, and the company had platted a new town several miles up-bay from the existing town.

that congressmen cooled by "glacial peaks of solid ice" would function better than those suffering from the notorious summer heat of the nation's capital. Three years later, Washington Senator Miles Poindexter also noticed the Mountain's glaciers, and recommended channeling their melt and runoff into a reservoir, then carrying it by tunnel through the Cascade Mountains and into Yakima Valley irrigation canals. En route it would flow through hydroelectric turbines. Farmers east of the mountains would benefit, and flooding and silting at Tacoma's harbor would be eased.

Hollywood discovered Rainier as a setting beginning in 1921. Directors chose the Mountain as a backdrop for silent films, and they continued to use it for such stars as Sonia Heine and Tyrone Power (*Thin Ice,* 1937), and Robert Mitchum (*Track of the Cat,* 1954). Heine and Power were in love—they welcomed time indoors while storms held up shooting. But after three weeks without sight of the Mountain, disheartened producers sent everybody home except for a skeleton crew. In his book *A Bird of Passage,* ski instructor Otto Lang tells of doubling for Heine. "Seen

Accepted altitudes have varied. The 1914 measurement of 14,408 feet held for forty-two years.

On the summit in 1956, Ranger Bill Butler cements in a new benchmark, raising the Mountain's official height to 14,410 feet. Rainier stands higher above its base than any other peak in the lower forty-eight states: 11,650 feet above Longmire. Four peaks are taller, but start from higher bases.

from the front and at a great distance, with a blond wig and a cute woolen ski cap propped on my head," he writes, "I could get away with this masquerade. The rear view was considerably less photogenic, especially at close range."

Native Americans on both sides of the Cascades have felt awe for the Mountain and gratitude for its resources, from huckleberries to mountain goats. In contrast, newly arriving explorers and settlers felt a need to quantify their admiration by measuring Rainier. Charles Wilkes was the first to do so. As leader of a U.S. Navy exploratory expedition in 1841, he was hosted at Fort Nisqually, a Hudson's Bay Company trading post south of today's Tacoma. While there, he measured Rainier's height by triangulation and announced 12,330 feet as the result. In ensuing years, readings of barometric pressure at the summit gave various heights; so did correlating elevation with the temperature at which water boiled. The loftiest of these measurements, 15,500 feet, was obtained in 1894 by Major Edward Sturgis Ingraham, a Seattle schoolteacher and a member of the state militia during the now infamous anti-Chinese riots of the mid 1880s. Inexperience with a barometer led Ingraham to disregard the effect of a storm engulfing the summit, and exuberance kept him from wondering why his reading exceeded others by about a thousand feet. Exuberance also prompted him to announce having determined "Columbia's Crest, the highest point in the United States excepting Mount St. Elias," an odd inclusion of the Territory of Alaska—and without mention of Mount McKinley, one-third higher than Rainier.

In 1913, using trigonometry, the U.S. Geological Survey recorded 14,408 feet as the height of Rainier. In 1956, using triangulation, they raised the figure to 14,410 feet. For this measurement, a helicopter lifted surveyors and instruments to the summit after the pilot insisted on lightening the aircraft by taking off the doors and remov-

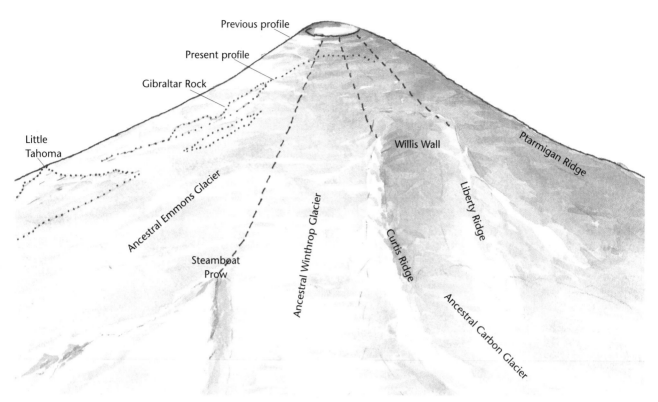

Previous profile

Present profile

Gibraltar Rock

Little
Tahoma

Ancestral Emmons Glacier

Steamboat
Prow

Ancestral Winthrop Glacier

Willis Wall

Curtis Ridge

Liberty Ridge

Ptarmigan Ridge

Ancestral Carbon Glacier

The presumed 16,000-foot height of Mount Rainier before the Osceola Mudflow is based on projecting remnant layers upward. But no one truly knows. Ice Age glaciers may have removed outermost layers. Also, the summit may not have been pointed and symmetrical.

ing the battery. Thin air offers little support for helicopter blades, but the pilot was determined to fly. Igor Sikorsky himself, designer of the helicopter and head of the aircraft company, stood waiting and watching in the parking lot at Paradise.

The 14,410-foot reading stood unchallenged until 1989. That year, the centennial of Washington's statehood, surveyors from a private company announced a measurement of 14,411 feet and 1 inch above sea level. They used Global Positioning System receivers to record satellite signals and computers to work out the mathematics. Nonetheless, the official height of the old volcano's summit remains 14,410 feet. The technology for the higher measurement was considered too new to be precise, and the company did not submit its data for peer review and analysis.

Until about 5,700 years ago, the Mountain truly stood higher, with its summit perhaps 16,000 feet above sea level. To visualize the mountain-that-was, mentally project upward the angles of exposed lava layers near today's top. Israel Russell, pioneering geologist who climbed Rainier in 1896, is the first to have done this. Most modern geologists agree with him regarding the probable height of the old top. Others disagree.

The Volcano

Mount Rainier is a young volcano, huge and high. Its fires are far from quenched; its glaciers are an awesome store of perched, frozen water. This combination is potentially hazardous. The peak belongs to a chain of fifteen recently active volcanoes stretched between Mount Garibaldi in southern British Columbia and Mount Lassen in northern California, part of the Pacific Ring of Fire. ("Recently active" in this case means within the last 4,000 years, less than a half tick of the geological clock.) Of these volcanoes, Rainier is the tallest and most imposing.

Across the Pacific, Japan's Mount Fuji at 12,388 feet is equally imposing, and is also a national park. Both volcanoes draw poets and painters and pilgrims to their slopes, and representatives of each have exchanged summit stones as tokens of good will. The Japanese consul in Seattle in 1935 accepted pumice from Rainier "encased in an Alaska Cedar cabinet," according to a report of Mount Rainier National Park's superintendent, and at about the same time, Japanese mountaineers "obtained a small stone on the summit of Mt. Fuji" and presented it to the American ambassador in Tokyo "encased in a cherry wood casket." After World War II, half of the ceremonial exchange had to be repeated. The Rainier stone was lost

Carolyn Driedger: Volcanoes

Carolyn Driedger began her career as a hydrologist by studying glacier ice. At Mount Rainier, she specialized in assessing recent glacier histories and the hazards of glacial outburst flows, and from those studies she developed, for the U.S. Geological Survey, a public-outreach program on volcanic hazards.

When I first noticed the Cascade volcanoes as an impressionable eleven year old, they seemed to me the most stunning features of all the natural world. Their snow-covered peaks appealed to my budding sense of aesthetics. As a young adult, I spent many happy hours skiing, climbing, and hiking on these majestic peaks. Any threats from volcanic activity were remote, a mere curiosity of thought.

My change in understanding began in 1980 when, as a new employee of the U.S. Geological Survey, I volunteered to help a colleague with fieldwork at Mount St. Helens, a volcano that clearly was awakening. During the afternoon of May 17th, 1980, my colleague Mindy Brugman and I delivered equipment to geologists at the Coldwater Ridge observation site just five miles north of the mountain. The air was clear and warm; the day and place seemed perfect for watching an eruption. We planned to stay overnight so as to ease logistics for Sunday morning's fieldwork, but David Johnston, a young volcanologist on duty, warned us not to do so unless absolutely necessary. Reluctantly, we admired the alpenglow on the volcano's snowy slopes, then drove down into the dark forests of the Toutle River valley and on via Interstate-5 towards our hotel in Vancouver.

At 8:32 the following morning we were heading back on Interstate-5 with Mount St. Helens in plain view when the cataclysmic eruption occurred. We watched amazed as the failure of the volcano's flank and the ensuing blast and eruption filled the sky with rock debris. It absolutely engulfed the volcano. We returned to Vancouver. Our colleague David Johnston, who had so accurately stated the hazards, was never seen again.

Recently, I've turned my attention to Mount St. Helens's neighbor to the north, Mount Rainier, and I've come to respect the sometimes bellicose behavior of both Northwest giants. Mount Rainier is older and higher than Mount St. Helens and has twenty-five times more permanent snow and ice. Combine this with Rainier's advanced age and the deteriorated state of its rock, and it's easy to see that huge landslides and lahars (volcanic mudflows) are not just possible, they're likely—someday. What's more, the population at risk is many times greater near Rainier than at Mount St.

Helens, and the economic stakes are much higher. New research indicates that Mount Rainier erupts more often than previously thought, and lahars can come with no warning. Part of my work is talking with people about the potential hazards. You wouldn't even have to be camped at Rainier, or in the direct path of a lahar, to be affected.

USGS scientists measure distance and angles from specific stations to certain points on the volcano, then compare current readings with baseline data to detect surface changes; this might foretell rising magma. They also record earthquakes, ground temperatures, and types and amounts of gas emissions. A new eruption typically would begin with steam blasts at the summit, which could escalate into a release of lava or ash.

When I visit Mount Rainier, its many scenic riches still easily lull me into a sense of calm. White snow glistens on upper slopes even in summer, and wild flowers wave in unison in the summer breezes. When I visit Mount St. Helens, I get a more ominous feeling. The breezes stir gusts of volcanic ash, which swirl around twisted tree trunks. The plants growing on the devastated terrain are pioneers—and look it. They contrast with the long-established plant communities at Mount Rainier.

It's more than thirty years since my first encounter with the Cascade volcanoes, and they now hold a new meaning for me. They aren't just objects of curiosity and admiration but are instead dynamic features with power to change form—and to change the lives of every being around them.

(Left) Six of Mount Rainier's twenty-five glaciers originate in the summit icecap, although volcanic heat keeps the crater's rim bare. Summer air temperatures range from minus 4° to 75° F. Winds reach 100 miles per hour. Steam vents register 191°F, the boiling point of water at the summit. (Top right) A climber explores a steam tunnel 100 feet below the surface of the west crater. (Bottom right) Illustration from an 1895 booklet

during the war. Before the war, English-language textbooks studied by schoolchildren had illustrated the section on America with photographs of New York, Chicago, and "Takoma-Fuji," as they called Mount Rainier.

The Mount Fuji stone, still in its cherry wood box, now sits in the office of 1990s Mount Rainier Park Superintendent Bill Briggle. He hopes for a formalized sister-mountain relation between the two "Fujis" and points out: "Both mountains symbolize beauty and strength, and the complexity of nature. And people from each nation already visit the other's mountain." With a sister relation, officials of the two parks could exchange practical information on handling today's great numbers of visitors, dealing with volcanic hazards, and protecting air quality in the parks. The Earth is one, and we all spin through space upon it together.

Overlapping craters, like saucers roughly a quarter mile wide, augment the broken summit of Mount Rainier. The rim of one crater is broken, the other intact. They belong to a cone built by continuing heat after the Mountain lost its old top. The eastern, younger crater formed about 1,100 years ago. Its circle of rock and rubble stays mostly bare year round because of fierce winds plus ground heat. Climbers can quickly resupply their drinking water by filling a bottle with snow and burying it, and anyone who sits down to rest in certain spots is likely to get right back up. In 1894 Frank Hawkins, who gave Columbia Crest its name, described "little steam jets as if emanating from hundreds of tea kettles. In some places the steam finds an outlet in small quantities, while in other places it comes spurting out from among the boulders in jets of considerable size."

Thermometers record subsurface ground temperatures approaching 200° Fahrenheit, and melt-tunnels and grottos riddle the snow that fills both craters to depths as great as 450 feet. These passages gape as much as 170 feet wide and have ceilings as high as a thirteen-storey building. One passage holds what may be the highest lake in the western hemisphere. In 1970 climbing guides Lou Whittaker and Lee Nelson threaded from rim to rim through the passages of the younger crater as part of a three-summer geophysical study sponsored by the National Geographic Society. They carried firemen's oxygen rebreather masks, in case of noxious fumes, but did not have to wear them. Bill Lokey of Tacoma, a professional emergency manager who has studied volcanic hazards and is an experienced mountaineer, served as field leader for the first two summers. On one occasion, wearing a wet suit, he found the maximum depth of the lake to be nineteen feet, and the water temperature barely above 32° Fahenheit. On another occasion, he and a companion accidentally broke their only light and groped through total blackness and hissing steam until they found a faint gleam of blue light from an opening. "When there's a wind on the surface, it creates a suction in the caves," Lokey explained in a Tacoma

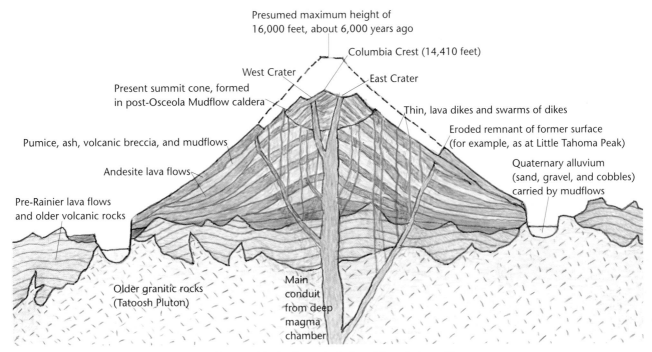

Generalized cross-section of Mount Rainier: Gases and hydrothermal solutions follow strata and fractures and cause rock to deteriorate. Water heated in the upper volcano circulates, some of it bubbling up as warm mineral springs at Longmire and Ohanapecosh.

News Tribune article. "As long as we kept that suction in our faces, we knew we were headed in the right direction."

Mount Rainier is sure to erupt again, though no one can say when. It may emit ash (finely fragmented rock), coarser pumice, or gases. It may emit lava. This present volcano, which had precursor volcanoes, first erupted half a million years ago. The most recent eruptions geologists can verify are explosions between 1820 and 1854. Their signature is a distinctive pumice found as much as six miles from the summit on Emmons Glacier moraines and a river terrace. By counting the growth rings of trees living on these sites, geologists can date when the surfaces must have formed. From that information, they can date the eruption, or eruptions. The physical evidence seems to corroborate historic accounts. John C. Fremont's journals of exploration mention an eruption at Mount Rainier in 1843, and, in his voluminous letters and reports, Tacoma civil engineer Fred Plummer refers to an eyewitness account by Native American John Hiaton in 1820, and to a report of volcanic activity in 1846.

In November 1894 unverifiable eruption reports commanded headlines in papers such as the Seattle *Post-Intelligencer* (P-I) and the Olympia *Washington Standard:* "Mount Rainier's Convulsions." "Say It Is Spouting." "Still in Eruption." Harry Surry, day-jailer at the Seattle police station, was the first to report the eruption. An ex-sailor, he was familiar with volcanoes, according to the *P-I,* because "once his ship lay becalmed three days in sight of Mount Aetna."

Surry told reporters: "Every morning when I get up I am in the habit of taking a look at the mountain . . . [and] at 6:20 a.m. . . . I saw a vast amount of black smoke arising from the southwestern part of the peak."

With that beginning, public excitement rose as high as the reported eruption. For days "the elements . . . prevented an observation of phenomenon at the summit." Nonetheless, conviction grew that the mountain was hiccoughing and had changed shape. Eyewitness observations at moments when the clouds lifted came from "teachers and children" at a school in Seattle's Fremont District, "which commands good views of the mountain" and from "a conductor on one of the Fremont [street]cars." Opera glasses and telescopes were at the ready, pointed toward Rainier, and even "incoming passengers on trains from Portland" were treated to a ten-minute pause "south of Tacoma in order to . . . witness the strange and awe-inspiring sight."

In December, the Seattle *Post-Intelligencer* sponsored a six-man snowshoe expedition to investigate the phenomenon. They traveled replete with seven "tried and true" homing pigeons and a roll of "fine oiled paper" for dispatches. On the ninth day, which was Christmas, the men turned back below Steamboat Prow at an elevation of about 9,000 feet. They confirmed thermal activity. "I saw three distinct columns of steam rise from the crater and dissipate in the air as they rolled upward," expedition leader Major Ingraham reported. "To the right of the steam

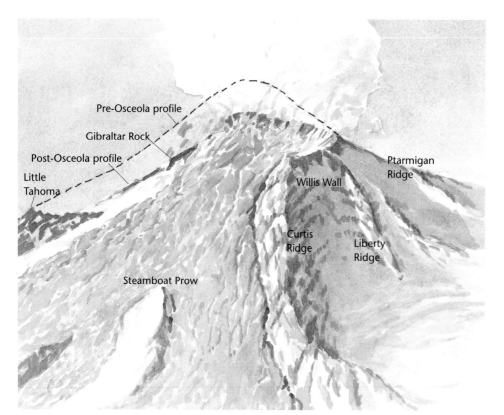

About 5,700 years ago steam eruptions and possibly also earthquakes triggered collapse of the summit and initiated the mammoth Osceola Mudflow, which reached Puget Sound, sixty miles distant. No mud-flows wreak havoc, willy-nilly. They follow predictable path-ways.

I observed a dark column of smoke that rose to a great height and then drifted away as the smoke coming from a chimney does. No, sir, there was no optical illusion. . . . Our chance for observation was good."

Fred Plummer, who had previously climbed the Mountain, wrote to the New York *Sun* that he regretted having missed a close-up view of an eruption and hoped "we will be treated to a first-class eruption in the near future, for there is nothing to be feared and much to be seen." That sanguine assessment is, of course, false. Eruptions are not sideshows.

Most likely, quakes centered beneath the volcano will herald future eruptions. For example, Mount St. Helens had more than a thousand quakes per week before it erupted in 1980. Rainier in the 1990s has had only about thirty quakes per year, indicators of continued volcanic life, but not necessarily forerunners of imminent eruption. Even so, Rainier is a "Decade Volcano," designated by the International Association of Volcanology and Chemistry of the Earth's Interior(!). It is one of fifteen such volcanoes worldwide, selected for ten years of intensive study because of the hazards they pose to large populations. More than others, these peaks are observed, sampled, measured, puzzled over, analyzed, diagnosed, and strategized. As knowledge advances, so do our concepts of living with a volcano.

One concept geologists are recognizing is that the Mountain has erupted more often and more explosively than was formerly believed. Eruption "events," as they are

Overlapping summit craters formed within the last 2,300 years. (They are shown here without their plugs of ice and snow.)

properly termed, have involved not only oozing or exploding lava but also steam emissions produced when groundwater or melt from snow and ice contact hot rocks. Fiery, roiling mixes of ash, gases, and rocks also have occasionally poured downslope, sending ash-laden hot winds ahead of them and devastating everything in their path.

In addition, other types of events may be linked to eruptions more often than was earlier believed, though such events also may occur without eruptions or movement of lava beneath the surface. The sulfurous gases that climbers notice wisping from rock crevices at the summit, and occasionally from glacier melt-holes, do more than simply rise into the air. They mix with underground water and steam to form hot acids that erode Rainier from the inside (a process called *hydrothermal alteration*). Layers of porous volcanic rock and rubble turn into clay. Parts of the Mountain lose strength and may collapse.

Spectacular rockfalls onto the Emmons Glacier in 1963 may have occurred in response to steam explosions, or they may have been due to hydrothermal alteration and gravity. Either way, a staggering twelve million cubic yards of rock dropped from Little Tahoma, the jagged satellite peak on Rainier's eastern flank. That much rock would cover a square mile twelve feet deep. It rode cushions of trapped air, much as experimental high-speed trains ride cushions of air. Traveling at seventy to ninety miles per hour, part of the rockfall rode over a small river-gauging structure causing little damage. It stopped half a mile short of the White River Campground. The entire event was a trifling one in Rainier's repertoire. It happened in December when no one was present to see it or be hurt by it,

although skiers at nearby Crystal Mountain heard its great booming and rumbling.

Millennia earlier and at a considerable distance from the Mountain, people surely did hear, see, and get hurt by a different type of event, the stupendous Osceola Mudflow, or *lahar*. The word comes from Indonesia, where volcanoes are common and such events frequent. Lahars are slurries of sediment, rubble, and rock which add trees and all else in their paths into their mix as they sweep across the land.

In the 1970s archaeologists excavating near Enumclaw found more than 300 stone scrapers, projectile points, gravers, drills, cobble tools, and charcoal from hearths lying about two feet beneath a clay-rich deposit unmistakably from Rainier. The deposit's composition matches material still pressed against the rock of Steamboat Prow at 9,700 feet on the northeast slope of the Mountain. This is the event that cost Rainier its top about 5,700 years ago and provided the snaggled platform for the present summit cone. Nobody knows the fate of the people of the tools. Probably they were living along the shore of a lake or marsh

Tokaloo Spire, seventy feet high on the uphill side, is part of the volcanic dike that fed the Klapatchee–St. Andrews lava flow. It is on the west side of the Mountain at 7,500 feet.

Telltale andesite columns along the trail to Emerald Ridge indicate rapid cooling of lava as its leading edge came in contact with glacier ice. Andesite lava is too viscous to flow far.

when the catastrophe struck. Escape by canoe or on foot seems unlikely. The lahar must have been moving at least fifty miles per hour. Even at fifty miles from the Mountain, it was carrying boulders three feet in diameter. Some people may have found themselves isolated on high ground surrounded by mud. Others must have died.

Geologists estimate that the Osceola lahar delivered about 3.8 cubic *miles* of clay, sand, gravel, cobbles, and boulders from the upper slopes of Rainier to the lowlands. It added ice and river water as it went, swelling the flow. The Osceola is one of the greatest lahars known anywhere. It was at least 500 feet deep as it passed the location of today's White River Campground. It poured 100 feet of mud, rock, and rubble across the Enumclaw plateau and wreaked change all the way to Puget Sound. Creeks and rivers were diverted, no longer flowing where they had the day before the lahar. Low hills disappeared. Small valleys were engulfed. Larger valleys were blanketed and widened. And sixty miles distant from the Mountain, what had been seawater at high tide and salt marsh at low tide instead became land. The Boeing Company and the city of Kent stand on Osceola debris; this is known from the records of wells drilled to below sea level. The farmers of the Puyallup Valley and Fife grow their strawberries and daffodils in soil that developed from the Osceola mudflow.

In 1898 geologist Bailey Willis, a member of the Geological Society of America, completed the first geologic map of Mount Rainier. He mistook the lahar deposit filling the Kent Valley for debris laid down by a retreating glacier, and half a century passed before geologists straightened out the mistake. In the early 1950s Dwight Crandell also mapped the area. He noticed a roadcut showing both a true glacial deposit and a layer of Osceola mud—two distinct deposits lying, one above the other, and soil separating the two. The glacial deposit had formed the surface of the land long enough for soil to develop, and vegetation had reclaimed the territory released by the ice. Then came the lahar. But how had it originated? "I could see Mount Rainier, but didn't make the connection for a long time," Crandell remembers. The mudflow remnant at Steamboat Prow fit that piece of the puzzle into place. A twig found in lowland Osceola deposits answered the question of when. It gave a radiocarbon date of 5,700 B.P. (before present). Volcanic ash of the same age pins the cause of the mudflow to an eruption.

Indian traditions tell of four whales living in a vast lake located in the area where Crandell did his mapping. For reasons that vary from version to version, they all decided to leave. They thrashed wildly and forced a channel from the lake to where Sumner is now, then swam along it and into Puget Sound. The water followed them. "Where the lake used to be is now a level valley," Upper Puyallup tribal elder Tom Milroy told anthropologist Arthur C. Ballard in the early 1900s. "That was when the world changed."

A mudflow 1,100 years ago ripped out and entombed trees in the Kent Valley, fifty miles from Rainier. Such flows may race twenty to forty miles per hour. Their steep, bouldery snouts head a churning mass of mud and rock. Their force leaves a swath of devastation.

Geologists know of at least sixty lahars from Rainier. They have swept down every one of the Mountain's valleys. In 1949, remnants of one literally spurted into public awareness in the Puyallup area. A magnitude 7.1 earthquake shook the town and startled homeowners by jiggling water from the pores of an underground layer and shooting it as much as six feet into the air. Sandy water suddenly erupted from lawns, forming geysers known as "sandblows." Liquefied sand welled up through a floor crack in the basement of one house and accumulated four feet deep. In fields, mounds of black sand gave the impression of invasion by an army of gophers. The character of the particles and the color of the sand were diagnostic. The sand had arrived in Puyallup 2,300 years earlier via a lahar from Rainier.

Evidence of another lahar, previously unsuspected, came to light as construction got underway at Emerald Downs Racetrack near Auburn in the mid-1990s. Bulldozers cut into a layer of sand studded like a raisin muffin with huge snaggled stumps and broken tree trunks. That brought geologists to have a look. They dated the lahar to 1,100 B.P. and found that it had been triggered by an eruption. The lahar's flow poured into Puget Sound at the mouth of the Duwamish River, near Seattle's present Terminal 107. That is sixty miles from Rainier, yet sand as much as twelve feet deep lies there. The flow was so great it probably also streamed into the Puyallup fork of the drainage.

Construction at another site also cut into lahar deposits in the mid-1990s. In this instance the deposits resulted from the well-known Electron Mudflow, which burst from

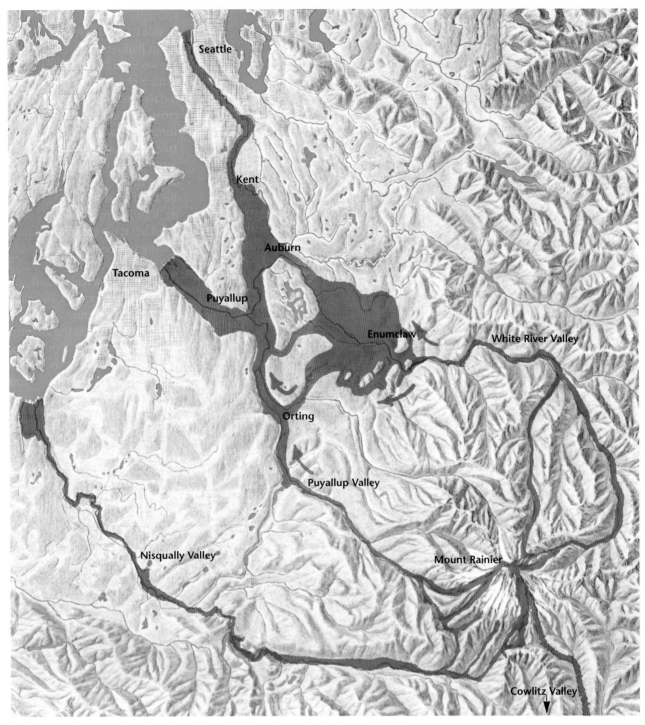

Pathways and extents of mudflows from Mount Rainier volcano during the past 5,700 years:
Major mudflows occur every 500 to 1,000 years; minor flows, several times a century.

Rainier's high western flanks 600 years ago. Geologists have known about this lahar for a long time, but the nature of science rests on always learning something more. Consequently, when Washington Department of Natural Resources geologist Patrick Pringle chanced upon a crew digging a sewer line near Orting, he stopped. "Geologists always look in holes," Pringle acknowledged. "And in this one there was a buried forest! Or there had been—a forest Pompeii, an old-growth forest with trunks six or seven feet in diameter."

Some trees stood broken but still rooted. Their bases were buried by mud and rock debris so deep it had raised the valley floor more than fifteen feet. Other trees had been ripped out by the force of the mudflow; some were abraded

15

John S. Fielding:
Tahoma Creek Rampage

While visiting the park from Denver, Colorado, John Fielding was caught by one of Tahoma Creek's outburst floods. This is his report to the National Park Service concerning the incident.

We arrived at the Tahoma Creek trailhead at about 9:30 a.m., June 29, 1987. It was a sunny day and the hike seemed like being in a magical forest, with trees as tall as I had ever seen and vegetation lush and green, as though we'd been transported to another planet.

Mary and I crossed the narrow, scary suspension foot bridge at about 11:00 a.m. We finished off the hike at the top of the trail where the view is Godlike: meadows covered with wild flowers and Mount Rainier right in your face.

We left this little paradise and came down the trail at about 2:00 p.m. Maybe two minutes before we got back to the suspension bridge, we heard a roar. The river really lit up with mist and dirt, and the ground was rumbling underfoot. When I turned the last switchback, the trees along the trail ahead were blowing and boulders the size of basketballs were flying over the bridge. . . . Mud, dirt, and wind were so thick you had to constantly rub your eyes to see.

I looked out over the bridge into the once-peaceful Tahoma Creek and saw an enormous, rushing wall of concretelike, brownish-black water with boulders the size of small houses being tossed downstream as though they were pebbles. I had never seen such force and devastation. Not even being in a typhoon in Asia during the war topped this sense of massive power and natural destruction. . . . When we had crossed the bridge on the way up, the creek was about 150 feet below us. Now it was a raging torrent just twenty feet below the bottom of the bridge, and with debris flying over the bridge.

Mary was about two minutes behind me, so when she caught up with me at the bridge, not knowing if we had seen the worst yet, I told her to try not to look down and to go as quickly as she could across the bridge. We made the crossing in what seemed like an eternity and we just missed getting hit by the larger rocks that were flying over us. We were only hit by a couple of the smaller rocks, and we were extremely lucky that we didn't just slip off the bridge, what with the mud and water that was on its surface. By the time we got across, our knees were weak. . . . If I had thought about it at all, we wouldn't have crossed.

almost in half by rocks and grit. Andesite boulders lay among the trees, rocks traceable to the Sunset Amphitheater near the summit of Mount Rainier. Cut off from oxygen and decay organisms, the wood had not rotted; Pringle cut several cross-sections with a chain saw, intending to count the rings and cross-date these trees with others. Beneath the bark of one cross-section he found a paper-thin ring just starting to form, indication that the lahar happened in spring. The tree must have died just as trilliums were starting to bloom, varied thrushes to sound their plaintive call, and sap to rise.

Indian people called the Orting area *swe'kW,* which, according to tribal member Tom Milroy, "means 'open,' because [a] flood cleared it and left it covered with porous stones." Villagers knew flooding was responsible because of a traditional account "that was not a *sXwiya'b* (myth)," Milroy said. "The man in the story was a real person. . . . He was out looking for *stL a'litu D* (magic power). He made five wedges of elkhorn. He went to the mountain, *T qo'b d,* and began to climb over the snow. He used the elkhorn wedges to chisel steps in the snow and ice." At the top, the man found a lake where he "swam and washed himself" and gained power. Then *T qo'b d* said to him, "You have come to stay one night—so I can talk." She told him that he would live long and when he died, her head would burst open "and the little lake will be released." And so it came to be.

Some lahars begin as floods unleashed from glaciers. These are called *jokulhlaups,* an Icelandic word. They start when blockage in the internal drainage system of a glacier suddenly clears and releases water. At Mount Rainier the two main triggers for these outbursts are heavy autumn rains or exceptionally hot weather, which greatly increases melt. Both situations pour water into cavities within the ice, or between it and bedrock—jokulhlaups waiting to happen.

At Rainier, the largest jokulhlaup in recent time was the Kautz Creek Flood of 1947. All who travel from Nisqually Entrance to Longmire cross its scar, now green with a young forest while still hosting stark remnants of the former forest. The October day of the flood, almost six inches of rain fell at Paradise in twenty-four hours, and a cloudburst evidently struck the Kautz Glacier. Concerned, Assistant Chief Park Ranger Bill Butler and a colleague checked the bridge by the Nisqually Glacier about ten o'clock that night; it had washed out during a previous heavy rain but this time it seemed all right. In Butler's words, they then decided to "take a run down to the entrance . . . and we noticed the Kautz was awfully riled up, pretty chocolate. Muddy looking." The men therefore swung the big gate at the entrance closed, hurried to Longmire to block the road there, and returned to Kautz Creek. "By that time the bridge was gone and the mud was just flowing across the

(Left) In 1947 water burst from the Kautz Glacier, unleashing a flood that covered the road and forest floor with mud. (Bottom left) Destruction of the bridge below the Nisqually Glacier in 1955 led to building the present high bridge. (Below) "A massive mud and rock flow changed a creek channel and moved boulders up to 12 feet in diameter." (caption from Seattle *Times* photograph of the Tahoma Creek Picnic Area, 1986)

road. . . . You could see these boulders suspended in the water, and mud about the consistency of concrete. The ground was quivering all over."

The flood lasted for twenty hours. It ripped ice from the center of the Kautz Glacier and cut a chasm below the terminus two and a half miles long and about sixty feet deep. It broke trees and toppled them. It also deposited a smothering blanket of silt and boulders which packed around roots and killed still more trees. By the time the event was over, half a mile of roadway had become useless and the riverbed behind the Nisqually entrance station had raised six feet. Downstream from the park, a third of the storage capacity of the reservoir behind Alder Dam had been filled, and silt was passing through the turbines.

On Tahoma Creek, one drainage west of Kautz Creek, jokulhlaups became almost standard beginning in 1967. The Park Service first closed a picnic ground, then closed all but the first few miles of the dead-end road along the west side of the park. At least twenty-three floods burst from the South Tahoma Glacier in the following two and a half decades, fifteen of them between 1986 and 1992. The Tahoma ice covers an area of about two and one half

square miles, double that of the better-known Nisqually Glacier. In 1967 water flowing from the surface of the ice at the 7,000-foot level cut the lower glacier in two and quickly became a wild, churning, concretelike mix carrying huge rocks and trees. Before the flood, hikers had crossed Tahoma Creek on a simple log bridge. By the early 1990s, they were crossing on a suspension bridge spanning a gorge 130-feet deep, cut by the repeated floods. Its depth had doubled in only six years.

No one can see beneath an entire glacier, but geologists think they know what causes the floods. Glaciers often flow over abrupt ledges and irregularities several tens of feet high. This leaves gaps between ice and rock. These pockets, which may be huge, fill with water. A sudden additional input increases pressure and creates a system of linked water-filled pockets and tunnels. Once these start to drain, the water bursts out in a series of great surges.

To keep constant surveillance over the combination of fire and ice at Rainier, and also to study other volcanic peaks, the U.S. Geological Survey created the Cascades Volcano Observatory in Vancouver, Washington. There, a

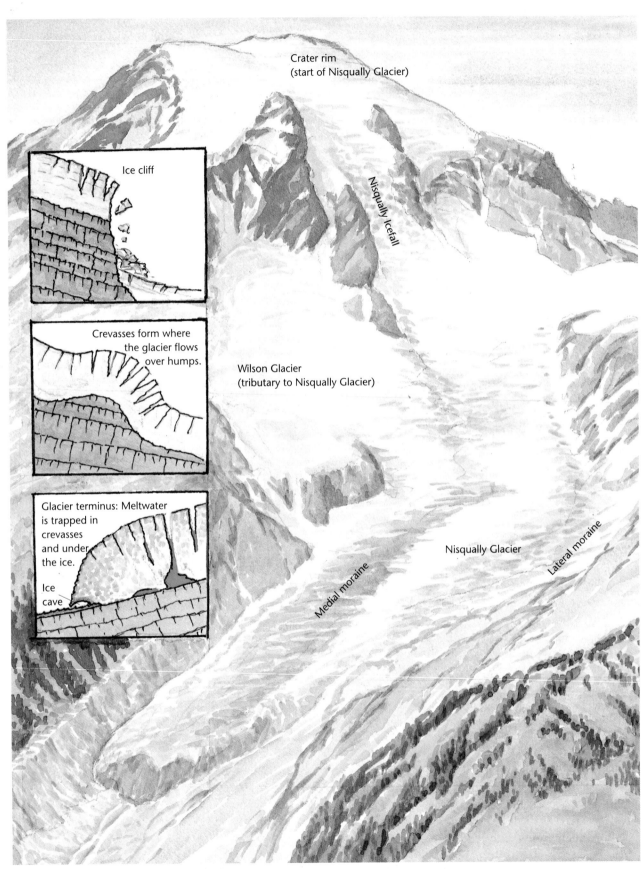

Crater rim
(start of Nisqually Glacier)

Nisqually Icefall

Ice cliff

Crevasses form where
the glacier flows
over humps.

Wilson Glacier
(tributary to Nisqually Glacier)

Glacier terminus: Meltwater
is trapped in
crevasses
and under
the ice.

Ice
cave

Nisqually Glacier

Medial moraine

Lateral moraine

Anatomy of the Nisqually Glacier: The Nisqually Glacier constantly advances, but it no longer fills the valley it previously carved. For centuries, it has been shortening at the snout and thinning overall, yet it still measures about 400 feet thick and three miles long.

Overall, the Nisqually Glacier moves downslope eight to eighteen inches per day, and in places as much as seventy-two inches. The lower reaches are mantled by rock fallen onto the surface.

SWAT team of geologists can mobilize within twenty-four hours and be underway to volcanic events anywhere in the world, carrying with them seismometers, geophones, theodolites, global positioning instruments, computers—and experience. Mount St. Helens's 1980 eruption gave birth to this unit. Its scientists work in partnership with University of Washington geologists who monitor seismic signals. These scientists watch wiggly lines drawn by pens connected to seismometers, which are placed at strategic field locations. They watch wiggles, but they *detect* slippage along a fault, the rise of magma, the release of a rockfall, the onset of a mudflow, even the step of a mountain goat close to a sensor.

Increasing knowledge links Mount Rainier's role as "the most hazardous volcano in the Cascades" into urban plans for the increasing human presence within its reach. Lahars and floods inevitably follow valleys; structures there could be vulnerable. Ash eruptions produce static electricity, which could disrupt radio transmissions. Ash clouds could ride prevailing winds and cause respiratory problems, choke engines, and pit windshields; travel by plane and automobile could be disrupted. Powerlines, over-weighted by clinging wet ash, could short out. Glowing lava reflecting at night on the underside of clouds might alarm city dwellers even at distances beyond its reach. Programs and publications explain such realities. Mayors, councils, and agencies plan with new awareness the sites of future airports, powerlines, highways, hospitals, schools, and suburbs.

At 1997 hearings concerning the national park's management plan for the next twenty years, Superintendent Bill Briggle was surprised at public reluctance to deal with the Mountain as a threat, even after having experienced Mount St. Helens's 1980 lesson in volcanic awakening. "The public wants access to Rainier as they now know it," he says. "We suggest closing the Longmire and White River campgrounds because they're in the path of past mudflows and floods and rockfalls, which may well happen again. The public says they prefer to take their chances. We suggest using shuttles to reduce some of the traffic congestion and help with an evacuation, if necessary. They want their cars. We have more data now, and scientists are learning still more. We must communicate it."

The upper Nisqually Glacier

Rivers of Ice

"It would be a matter of interest to the Mazamas to contribute to the solutions of the problem of variation of glaciers by observing and recording the changes which occur among the glaciers of Oregon and Washington." So wrote glaciologist Harry Fielding Reid, in the 1903 journal of the Mazamas, a Portland outdoor club. At the time, many Americans assumed that trips to the European Alps or the wilds of Alaska were the only way to see true glaciers. Yet Mount Rainier had twenty-eight named glaciers (now dwindled to twenty-five, owing to melt). First-hand accounts of journeys to see the Mountain's ice easily commanded attention in Puget Sound newspapers. The Tacoma *Daily Ledger* for June 23, 1883, described the impressions of a distinguished party that included U.S. Senator George Edmunds, vice president of the Northern Pacific Railroad T. F. Oakes, and Western Division Assistant Manager J. M. Buckley. They had gone up the Carbon River Valley, and

they remarked on the vast forest they passed through and the house of Bailey Willis, "dimensions 15 × 30 × 9, built from the butt of one cedar, which tree was only one of many in the immediate neighborhood." But it was the ice that held their full attention. Indeed, the report concluded, the men all "agreed without a dissenting voice, that there was not a scene comparable to those glaciers [anywhere else] on this continent. . . . They would not have missed the trip for ten times the amount of fatigue entailed."

Sixteen years later the glaciers were a major reason for establishing the Mountain as a national park, and they would remain its most touted feature for years. The *National Park Portfolio,* published in 1916 by the Department of the Interior to promote tourism, focuses most of its Rainier text on glaciers. It barely mentions flowers, forests, and other attractions. The Mountain is a "frozen octopus" with "icy tentacles." It has glaciers "roaring over precipices like congealed water falls." The Nisqually Glac-

(Left) Seattle Mountaineers expeditions introduced hundreds of Northwesterners to Rainier's glaciers.

(Left below) Eugene Ricksecker designed the road to Paradise to pass within a thousand feet of the Nisqually Glacier terminus. When the road finally reached that far in 1908, he reported: "A few minutes' walk brings one within pale of [the glacier's] icy breath and touch of its icy cold." Since then the Nisqually has retreated almost half a mile.

ier is "glistening white and fairly smooth at its shining source on the mountain's summit," but its lower reaches are "soiled with dust and rent by terrible pressure into fantastic shapes."

For a volcano to be sheathed in ice seems incongruous: heat intense enough to melt rock juxtaposed with glaciers? Yet even before the Rainier volcano finished building, glaciers began sculpting its lofty flanks. They formed not because of arctic cold but because of superabundant snowfall. Only two conditions are needed. More snow must fall in winter than melts in summer, and there must be enough time for it to compact into ice and start flowing because of gravity and its own weight. This critical depth varies from several tens of feet to 200 or more, depending on exact conditions and slope. The Nisqually moves downslope an average of eight to eighteen inches per day, and as much as seventy-two inches per day in its thickest and steepest portions.

In the 1890s and early 1900s, most women visiting Rainier hiked and climbed in skirts, although those who were more boldly daring wore loose bloomers.

Crevasses form because glacier ice flows not as a viscous fluid, like asphalt, but as a solid. It follows the same laws of physics that govern, for example, the bending of iron. Stressed too far, it splits. The splits—crevasses—are a by-product of the glacier's accommodation to rock knobs and ridges at its bed, and to different rates of internal flow within the ice. Bottom ice moves more slowly than upper ice. Crevasses form. They seem almost bottomless to anyone standing at the lip and peering in for the first time, but pressure actually limits the crevasses to little more than 100 feet deep. Beyond that, they squeeze shut.

(Above) By dropping onto the Nisqually Glacier above Paradise, climbers can sample the unique beauty of crevasses without expending the time or energy needed for the summit. The snowfalls of successive winters show as layers in crevasse walls.

(Right) Mountain guide Lou Whittaker belays a climber who is demonstrating self-rescue from a crevasse as part of a week-long climbing and photography seminar high on Mount Rainier.

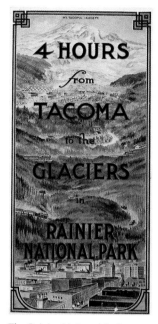

The Rainier National Park Company promoted travel with booklets ranking the Mountain's glaciers as a chief attraction.

(Above) In his account of climbing Mount Rainier in 1888, John Muir told of driving caulks into the soles of his shoes, then, "set[ting] forth afresh, slowly groping our way through tangled lines of crevasses, crossing on snow bridges here and there after cautiously testing them, jumping at narrow places, crawling around the ends of the largest. . . . It was nerve-trying work."

(Left) Rock fragments frozen into the bottom of glaciers scratch, polish, and gouge the bedrock they pass over. Ice alone would be too soft to do this. At Rainier, Box Canyon (on the Stevens Canyon road between Paradise and Ohanapecosh) is an easy place to see such scratches. Worldwide, glacier erosion in rock dates to at least two billion years ago.

Throughout the Pleistocene epoch, which included the most recent Ice Age, Rainier received vast quantities of moisture from the Pacific, borne by westerly winds and precipitated as snow. Thus nourished, glacier tongues radiated as much as sixty-five miles from the Mountain, gouging bedrock with sharp-edged fragments of rock held in an icy grip, and grinding and polishing because of sediments frozen into the bottom of the ice like sandpaper.

In the Nisqually Valley, the town site of Elbe lay beneath Pleistocene ice a quarter mile thick. At White River, the site of the present campground lay beneath ice a half mile thick. The glaciers produced sheer headwalls as high as 3,000 feet, and they broadened and deepened pre-existing, V-shaped stream valleys. New flows of lava might destroy parts of the icy mantle, and titanic bursts of steam might fracture it, but all such events were inconsequential. Climate dictates the waxing and waning of glaciers. When it warms enough that melt-rates exceed snowfall, glaciers retreat. When it cools enough that snow accumulation exceeds melt, glaciers advance. Scientists believe that if Rainier's present ice were somehow stripped away, it would re-form. The Mountain's slopes are directly in the path of clouds moving inland from the Pacific and are cold. Mid-elevations actually receive more snow than does the summit. Clouds rise only as much as is necessary to clear the barrier of the Cascade range, and the Mountain's top often protrudes above them. Snowfall is greatest at elevations of 5,000 to 8,000 feet, not at the top.

23

About thirty-four square miles of Mount Rainier's slopes remain white at summer's end, a greater area of ice and snow than that of all the other Cascades volcanoes combined. The Carbon Glacier is almost six miles long and is 700 feet thick at its center. It reaches farther down the valley than Rainier's other glaciers, which in 1899 made it a commercial temptation for entrepreneurs. The *Daily Ledger* on December 14th published an article headlined: "MOUNT TACOMA ICE. A Rather Novel Plan to Bring It Here." The article that followed quoted Northern Pacific "Division Superintendent Horner," who announced that "prominent men of this city and a number of capitalists in New York [plan] to supply the city with absolutely pure ice" from the Carbon Glacier. "It is frozen way up in mid-air where no spurious gases ever corrupt its purity and where it is impossible for decaying vegetation to taint it. No city in the world could get purer or better ice. . . . The company proposes to utilize the timber, which is so plentiful and can be had for nothing, and build a chute and send the ice down the side of the mountain and through the valley to Tacoma and adjacent cities and villages." This was an era when ice supplied the only refrigeration. Delivery from the chute to the city presumably would be via Northern Pacific rails; they stretched between Tacoma and Wilkeson, a few miles from the glacier. The plan never was instituted.

Rainier's glaciers are retreating, as are temperate glaciers throughout the world. "They're going extinct," sighs glaciologist Austin Post, whose aerial photography has kept watch on ice from the Andes to the Aleutians since the 1950s. "Our prettiest glaciers are threatened." Warming climate is the reason. Perhaps as much as half of the ice present in temperate regions at the beginning of the twentieth century has melted. Many glaciers have entirely disappeared. Rainier's Paradise Glacier has shrunk. It was probably the Mountain's most beloved ice because of exquisitely beautiful melt tunnels formed by warm air moving along the melt stream. Now the tunnels are gone, a scenic loss, as was the loss decades earlier of ice tunnels at the snout of the Nisqually Glacier. Of greater consequence, however, is the effect on future water supplies. The loss of glacier ice will be felt by urban water users long accustomed—without thinking about it—to current rates of melt.

During the 1950s and again in the mid-1970s, some of Rainier's glaciers thickened and sent waves of active ice overriding stagnant, older ice. This produced net advances at the snout, but they were short-lived responses to climate fluctuations. The overall pattern is retreat. The Nisqually Glacier has withdrawn almost a mile since Professor Joseph LeConte of the University of California made the first measurements in 1907. The record ranks the Nisqually as the longest-monitored glacier in the

Glacier meltwater runs milky with silt and clay, a characteristic that distinguishes glacier-fed streams from those carrying snow melt.

western hemisphere. Photographs from the late 1800s and early 1900s show the terminus about a quarter mile below the site of the present Nisqually River bridge. Now the glacier is out of sight from the bridge and its lower reaches are so smothered by rock they no longer look like ice. The trail to its terminus has been long closed, owing to the danger of rockfall.

Native Americans saw Rainier's shifting white cloak and had a story explaining it. An unidentified "old Puyallup Indian" told the story to F. H. Saylor, purser on a Puget Sound steamer, who published it in 1899. The story tells that once, when the Great Spirit was readying the world, *Do-ce-wallops* had two wives whose jealousy upset him so much he started mistreating his people. Because of this behavior, the Great Spirit stepped in and "*Ta-ho-ma* [Mount Rainier, one of the wives] was changed into a mountain as a warning to wives—a warning that would always be in view—of what jealousy would bring to them. Around her form [the Great Spirit] wrapped a mantle of white and cold, ever keeping the fire of jealousy within from busting forth to cause harm, as she had done before."

In the 1950s the main tunnel of the Paradise Ice Cave extended nearly half a mile, formed by warm air entering along the glacier's meltstream. In 1971 the Park Service closed the cave as unsafe. By 1991 its ceiling had collapsed.

Blue light waves pass through ice, turning glacier cave walls blue; other wavelengths are absorbed and not visible. Trapped air forms bubbles as snow compacts into ice.

Floyd Schmoe: Centenarian

Floyd Schmoe, born in 1895, worked at Mount Rainier as winter caretaker, climbing guide, ranger, and park naturalist. A peace activist, he has been nominated three times for the Nobel Peace Prize and was awarded Japan's highest civilian honor for his work helping to rebuild Hiroshima. His book, A Year in Paradise, *has become a classic. The following remarks are from a 1998 interview with Seattle's KCTS television producer Jean Walkinshaw.*

I came to Seattle in 1917 from Kansas, where the highest thing I'd ever seen was a windmill. As I looked across the University of Washington campus and saw the Mountain, I was immediately fascinated by its immense presence. I thought: the first afternoon I have off, I'll take a hike out there. I was surprised to find it was seventy miles away, and I didn't get there for a while.

I was in the College of Forestry, and one of the students told me that he had worked summers at Mount Rainier National Park and that it's a pretty good job. I went immediately down to Tacoma, where the headquarters of the Park Company was, and I did a little name-dropping about the climbing I'd done in the Alps while I was over there during the First World War, and I asked the company's general manager, Mr. Martin, for a job as guide. He said that wouldn't be needed till mid-July, but if I really wanted work he could send me up to shovel snow off Longmire Inn. So I came back to Seattle, and by the next day or two, I was up there shoveling snow.

Floyd Schmoe's sketches: Pack rat ("Moving their chattels from room to room, they are damnably annoying in the dead of night."); Steamshovel clearing the road after the long winter

Caretakers at Paradise Inn have lived for entire winters beneath a blanket of snow thirty feet deep.

About that time, Mr. Martin called and said the winter keepers at Paradise Inn, seven miles up the mountain by trail, had disappeared. After a batch of home brew they didn't get along very well, and they'd chased each other out of the park. No one ever saw them again. They didn't even stop in Tacoma for their paycheck. So Mr. Martin said, if I'd like to pick up Ruth [Schmoe's wife], we could go to Paradise Inn as winter keepers for the rest of the year.

I did a lot of very bad skiing that winter. We didn't have ski boots. We just strapped skis onto our feet, and as we were all alone on the mountain, I'd go down to Longmire on skis, carrying a pair of webs [snowshoes] on my back. It would take me only about forty minutes to get down, but with a heavy load of fresh food, it would take about four hours to get up to Paradise again.

I became a ranger after finishing college in 1922. Two years later I qualified as park naturalist, and I was only the second park naturalist in the whole Park Service. Yellowstone already had one. I was the first at Rainier.

For the almost 103 years that I have lived, the Mountain has always been an important part of my life. I lectured across the country when the Park Service was promoting parks. They're running travel down now because there are too many people, but they paid me to go east and show slides and so forth. I'd say that Mount Rainier is a volcano with glaciers and, like it, we should have a warm heart and a cool head. That's something I've always aspired to.

A blowing snowstorm adds to the white blanket enveloping the Paradise Visitor Center. Occasionally such storms occur even in July.

Snow Blanket

Paradise, at an elevation of 5,400 feet on the Mountain's southern flank, holds the North American record for snowfall: 1,122 inches between July 1971 and July 1972. Nearly 100 feet! In ordinary years, half this much falls, then drifts and packs to depths of twenty to thirty feet. Beneath such a blanket Floyd Schmoe and his wife Ruth lived as caretakers for Paradise Inn in the winter of 1920. A graduate student at the University of Washington, newly married, and flat broke, Schmoe signed on for the job without knowing the inn was completely buried "and each of its hundred or more rooms was as dark as midnight even on the brightest day." His book, *A Year in Paradise*, tells of snowshoeing with his wife the last mile and a half to their winter home, "two tiny black dots on a great white field." Arriving, "all that we saw were a few feet of the two massive stone chimneys protruding from a mound in the endless expanse of snow. . . . It was hard to realize that these chimneys, from which no welcoming smoke appeared, lay buried in the drifts below them."

The hotel bakery became the couple's kitchen, the pantry their larder. Under the snow they could not hear the wind that pummeled the Mountain with storms. The building "would creak and groan every night as the snow settled and bore down upon it," yet with Coleman lanterns, candles, and an airtight wood stove, "it was really quite cozy on long winter evenings."

Few humans live as snow troglodytes, but for many organisms snow is an essential home. Marmots and golden-mantled ground squirrels wait out the winter by hibernating under its blanket. Their body temperatures drop close to that of their burrows, their heart rates slow to four

Flamboyant park-company publicity included this photograph and caption: "A pony guide rides his mount over the snow tunnel entrance at Paradise Inn. Summer suns do not destroy the tunnel until July."

or five beats per minute, and their respiratory rates slow to about one breath per minute. Hibernation is not a form of sleep. It is more like being anesthetized or in a hypnotic trance, although infinitely deeper. Metabolism plummets. Glands operate differently. Hormones produce effects not duplicated in active life. Only about one-hundredth of normal nutrition is needed, an amount small enough to be supplied by stored fat.

Bears semihibernate without entering a truly comatose state; they briefly venture into the surface world on sunny days. Foxes and snowshoe hares never leave the surface world. During storms a fox will simply curl its bushy tail across its nose and disappear beneath the falling snow. A hare will take shelter at the base of a tree or bush. Ptarmigan, the largest year-round birds of the subalpine community, change their plumage from mottled brown to camouflage white and dive—or merely snuggle—into winter's white fluff. On their legs and feet they grow veritable snowshoes: feathers fold out of the way as the foot is

(Left and below) Wet snow and little wind turn winter trees to plumes of white. At first some flakes slide off the needles, others melt or ricochet. But once they begin to stick, they accumulate rapidly.

(Right) Nisqually River below Glacier Bridge

Snowpacks are dynamic. Flakes lose their points, become rounded, and fit more closely together. Crusts form, break down, and re-form. Temperatures fluctuate. And each fresh snowfall starts the process anew. Without snow's insulation, many plants and animals would die in winter.

lifted, drag against the snow, and increase the bearing surface with each forward step.

Pikas, which are relatives of the rabbit, stay active in rocky crannies beneath the snow. They feed almost hourly on the meadow "hay" they cut, sun-cure, and store during the summer. Its nutritional value is too meager to sustain body temperature without the near-constant feeding. For pikas, escape from winter is impossible by traveling to lower country. Nor can they add enough fat or fur to protect themselves. Without snow, they would die. The same is true for mouselike voles, which survive the cold by staying active beneath the snow. There the ground is too well insulated to freeze deeply, and plant stems and roots and bulbs are available as winter food. After the snow has melted, the voles' foraging paths remain on the ground surface like curious, snakelike accumulations of plant leftovers.

New-fallen snow is virtually a froth—perhaps nature's greatest insulating material. The generality is that ten inches of snowfall equal one inch of moisture, but Rainier's snow is so wet that the ratio probably is lower. Change within the snowpack is constant. Air gets squeezed out as snow crystals start rounding and settling. Pores and hollows fill in and density increases. Snow layers close to the ground hold in heat given off by the Earth and develop

depth hoar. Its loose lattice of crystals shatters readily and lets the voles and their ilk scamper about relatively freely at the ground surface.

Other creatures live their entire lives in, on, and under snow. They know no other environment. Snow worms are an example. Poet Robert Service immortalized them in his depiction of the Canadian Yukon, and summer rangers at Rainier at least once, to their embarrassment, found worms in the bottom of guests' glasses after having used snow to chill drinks. Relatives of earthworms, snow worms look like inch-long brown or black threads. Sometimes they writhe by the dozen—or even the hundreds—on glaciers and snow patches.

Algae provide food for the worms. They turn late-summer snow patches pink, or even red—a surprise for hikers new to the Northwest. The algae apparently overwinter in the ground, then develop hairlike flagella and swim to the surface to resume active life. Some combination of summer melt and light stimulates them. As their numbers swell, they not only color the snow but make it smell like watermelon—albeit without the taste. In 1818 Arctic explorer John Ross found pink snow on Baffin Island and took samples back to London. No one knew what caused the color.

Insects blow onto Rainier's slopes, most of them dead on arrival, or soon to become so. They are the chance victims of wind. Some are carried up from surrounding forests, some from the agricultural fields of eastern Washington. Scavengers and predators feed on them and on pollens and spores, also delivered by wind—a smorgasbord of organic tidbits. These arthropod gastronomes range from wolf spiders to midges and springtails (which have an appendage under their abdomens that springs open and launches them the equivalent of a 150-foot jump for a human). Body chemistries with peptide and glycerol antifreezes protect tissues from rupturing despite minus-zero temperatures, and radiant energy from the sun helps offset the chill. Sunlight comes from above and also reflects from the myriad glistening surfaces of snow grains—lifesaving for otherwise frigid snow creatures, but a painful reality for climbers who forget to smear sunscreen under their chins.

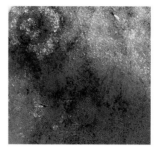

Rainier's snow hosts several life-forms, including minuscule worms, wolf spiders, and a kind of algae that turns the snow pink.

In the high country, one winter's snow may still linger when the next winter's snow starts to fall.

Rosy finches, pipits, ptarmigan, and other birds find enough food to warrant regularly foraging high-elevation snowfields. Ravens somehow know when female flying ants and other large insects blow onto the snow. Deer mice occasionally surprise climbers at Camp Muir, at the 10,000-foot level of the Mountain. They may readily find enough crumbs and insects to subsist on, but how do such small mammals reach that elevation? A porcupine strayed as high as Disappointment Cleaver above Camp Muir in 1947. And a bear was seen by climbers on the Emmons Glacier early one morning and by other climbers at midday on the Kautz Glacier—literally, the bear that went over the mountain.

Sooty grouse

Ptarmigan

Summer's Rush

Summer comes late to the high country and leaves early. Result? Plants above 5,000 feet do not place their entire faith in seeds. They may set seed, but no high-country species relies on starting over each year. There is not enough time between one year's melt and the next year's snow; plants survive as perennials rather than by testing fate as annuals. Most hold stem and leaf buds barely within the soil or just above its surface, protected by snow from freezing and perfectly positioned for renewed growth as soon as the world shrugs off its white mantle.

In an experiment, plants once were moved from lowlands near the Tyrolean Alps to upper slopes as a means of studying how they would adapt to a mountain environment. As expected, most died, but plants that lived developed shorter stems, greener leaves, brighter petals, and earlier bloom. Their lowered growth reduced exposure to wind and optimized use of warmth from the ground. Their deepened pigmentation accelerated absorption of the

sun's rays. By speeding life processes, the plants increased their odds of leafing out, growing, and flowering within the time available. Some of Rainier's subalpine plants put out only two or three leaves per year and lengthen their stems by the merest fraction of an inch. But they have long roots. A moss campion two inches high may be rooted more than a foot deep. It needs such deep roots as an anchor against wind and sliding soil. Root depth would be a waste if water were the purpose; water tends to be available near the surface.

Avalanche lilies have perfected the art of coping. Each September, as other plants are shutting down for winter, these lilies start growing at the tips of their bulbs. They anticipate summer. When it actually approaches, they perform an extraordinary juggling of metabolism and literally melt their way up through thinning snow. Stored carbohydrates permit this burst of energy. They raise the temperature of the plant and also warm the air in the melt-hole enough to let photosynthesis begin.

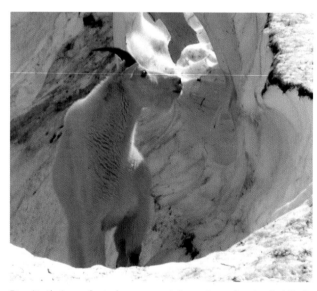

Despite their surefootedness, mountain goats are frequently killed in falls or by getting caught in avalanches.

To escape the torment of biting flies, deer stop grazing the flowery meadows to seek rest on snowbanks.

The avalanche lilies are a signal. Summer has arrived in the high country. It comes with a glorious rush, a sort of biotic urgency that skids over spring and flings out all possible warm-weather splendors at once. Water that had dripped and trickled suddenly cascades, and marsh-marigolds bloom—creamy and golden—submerged in its eddies. Waterfalls spill from cliff tops. Lakes thaw, briefly host icebergs, then take on the sparkling blue of summer. Mother bears venture out with their cubs. Marmots shriek odes to the worth of risking danger from eagles rather than miss a moment's sunshine.

Although deserts may seem the quintessential harsh environment, Rainier's high meadows are equally demanding. Hard-core adaptations gird their gentle look.

Avalanche lilies are among the first high-country flowers to bloom each summer. Light penetrates two to three feet into snow, permitting photosynthesis to begin.

Martha Falls, in upper Stevens Canyon: When winter loses its grip and the yearly thaw at last begins, creeks, rivers, and waterfalls splash noisily back to life.

Thin soils and exposure to sun and wind mean difficult growing conditions for sub-alpine meadow species. Paint-brush semi-parasitizes the roots of other plants, stealing their moisture and nutrients for itself.

Nature writer John Muir in 1888 described Paradise as "the lower gardens of Eden . . . filled knee-deep with fresh, lovely flowers of every hue, the most luxuriant and the most extravagantly beautiful of all the alpine gardens I ever beheld in all my mountain-top wanderings." Perhaps too many people have agreed with him. Only one century separates Muir's Eden from today's all-too-real problems owing to the excess of one species: people. More than a million visitors a year now come to Paradise. Twelve miles of maintained trails lead through flowers and to vantage points, but mixed with them are shortcut trails, abandoned horse trails, old roads, former campgrounds, and scars from the rope tows of a ski operation. Damage from the horse trails is the most severe. The riding concession closed in 1965, but a full quarter-century later some trails still cut glaring swaths five to ten feet wide with foot-deep ruts.

Through the years, piecemeal efforts attempted to correct such flaws, but not until the 1980s was a systematic plan worked out. National Park Service rangers, botanists, sociologists, interpreters, a landscape architect, a trail crew foreman, and volunteers set to work. Their first step was to analyze why trampling continued despite efforts to discourage it. For example, barriers closing off an area to allow plants to recover were being ignored. So uniformed rangers strolled the trails. They asked questions. They listened. People said they recognized yellow polypropylene rope as a barrier, but not split-rail fences. In cities, yellow ropes closed off critical areas; the park's rail fences seemed bucolic, even decorative. Signs that admonished "Protect the Meadows. Stay on Paved Trails." conveyed nowhere near the punch of "Off-Trail Hikers May Be Fined." One family seated in the flowers explained they were not walk-

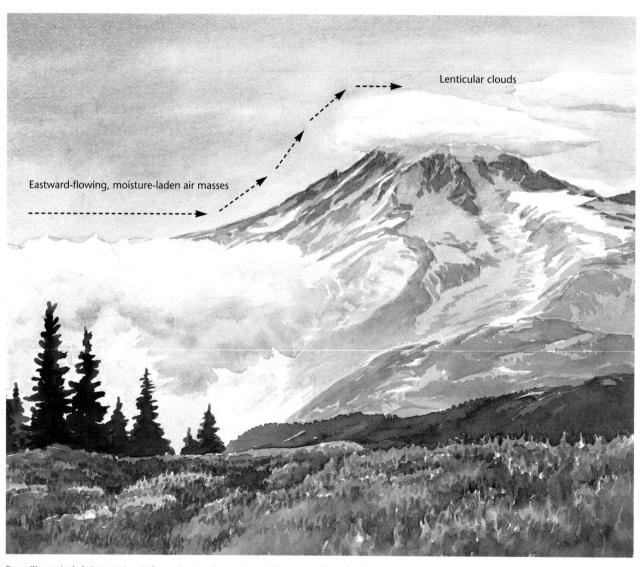

Lenticular clouds

Eastward-flowing, moisture-laden air masses

Prevailing winds bring moist air from the Pacific to Mount Rainier, resulting in deep winter snow.
In summer, clouds often "cap" the summit by dissipating to lee as rapidly as they form to windward.

"An obvious little sign at Tipsoo Lake where Winter lingers deep and long," the photographer wrote in his album.

Volunteer work in 1997 totaled more than 52,000 hours. In the subalpine meadows alone, fourteen volunteer groups that year contributed 1,800 hours to loosen compacted soil, construct erosion barriers, fill ruts, set out plants, and sow seeds and lay temporary protective covers of excelsior netting over them. At Yakima Park, they lifted 4,755 plant clumps from the mile-long road to a campground closed twenty-five years ago, covered them with burlap, and left them in a tree while National Guardsmen recontoured the land, using heavy equipment flown in by Guard helicopter crews. Then they replanted all that they had salvaged.

At Sunrise, 1990s volunteers helped park botanists collect seeds, which were sprouted in the park greenhouse and then replanted, also by volunteers, as part of a revegetation project.

ing off the trails, but picnicking. Photographers denied they were trampling; they were looking for a camera angle.

Inventive excuses called for inventive solutions. Interpretive panels explaining meadow ecology went up, and, as a training mission, army helicopter crews lifted handsome wooden benches and large rocks into position along trails to invite rest and contemplation. Botanists and volunteers turned their attention—and aching backs—to replanting scars at Paradise and Yakima Park, on opposite sides of the Mountain.

In 1990, friends of a Rainier aficionado celebrated her fiftieth birthday by laboring for a weekend in the meadows. They have returned every summer since. So have a host of other volunteers, about half of them as individuals, half from organizations such as Elderhostel, Boeing Management Association, the Native Plants Society, Garden Clubs of America, Canon USA (the copy machine company), "Good Neighbors" from Target stores, the crew of the U.S.S. Rainier (a supply vessel that comes to Bremerton every year), Boy Scouts, Girl Scouts, and environmental science classes from schools in the surrounding area. University students in Tokyo have even paid their own way from Japan to volunteer at Rainier; Superintendent Briggle was the only national park superintendent in the United States to answer a Waseda professor's letter asking about such an opportunity for his students. Briggle knew that Renton resident Dixie Gatchell, the volunteer who manages the program, would find a task for them. Her computer file of Volunteers in Parks holds almost a thousand names, and a website (www.nps.gov/volunteer) posts openings for more. Opportunities range from carpentry and painting to engineering, giving roadside assistance to motorists, acting as campground hosts, and patrolling the backcountry.

Recent study has found that some heather communities at Mount Rainier are 10,000 years old.

anemone   phlox   avalanche lily   silky phacelia

Meanwhile, the park horticulturist tended meadow cuttings and germinated seeds in the "re-veg greenhouse" at park headquarters in Ashford—which operates something like a hatchery, but for plants instead of fish or chickens. Seeds and young plants start in the warm greenhouse, but soon are moved outdoors. It would not do for them to get used to the good life only to be released back into their natural, high, harsh environment. Greenhouse success sent 40,000 two- to three-inch transplants back to subalpine meadows in addition to the 4,755 salvaged at the former campground. Fifth-grade students from the Ashford school help with this ongoing work.

Part of the restoration program's success depends on heeding the genes that have evolved to meet meadow realities—and this may represent an exceedingly long time. For example, botanist Ola Edwards has made the astonishing discovery that Rainier's heather communities are truly ancient. Individual plants may live fifty years and may take two centuries to become established as a community. Once successful, the community endures. Edwards collected buried stems from beneath pink and cream and white heather mats and sent them off to be carbon dated. Back came the report: more than 7,000 years old. Corroboration of the date came from beneath some of the heather patches: a layer of volcanic ash from Oregon's Mount Mazama, which blew its top and formed Crater Lake 7,000 years ago. The ash lay as a thin white line, well *above* the base of the debris of heather stems and seed capsules underlying today's living plants. That total accumulation is over three feet deep: today's heather meadow is growing on top of its ancestors from 10,000 years ago. Bees are pollinating heather blossoms located in the same places where Rainier ancestor-bees were pollinating ancestor-heather while the Bering Land Bridge still connected Siberia to Alaska. Few plant communities on Earth can claim such antiquity.

(Left to right) arnica and paint-brush, anemone seedheads, marsh marigold

(Below) By September, high-country meadows replace their robe of flowers with the reds and yellows of huckleberry, willow, and mountain ash.

Denise Levertov: Three Ways of Looking at a Mountain

During the last decade of her life, poet Denise Levertov (1923–97) made her home along the southwestern shore of Lake Washington in Seattle, where she could see the Mountain from her windows. The following poems are from her book Evening Train *(1992), reprinted here by permission of New Directions Publishing Corporation.*

Settling

I was welcomed here—clear gold
of late summer, of opening autumn,
the dawn eagle sunning himself on the highest tree,
the mountain revealing herself unclouded, her snow
tinted apricot as she looked west,
tolerant, in her steadfastness, of the restless sun
forever rising and setting.
                    Now I am given
a taste of the grey foretold by all and sundry,
a grey both heavy and chill. I've boasted I would not care,
I'm London-born. And I won't. I'll dig in,
into my days, having come here to live, not to visit.
Grey is the price
of neighboring with eagles, of knowing
a mountain's vast presence, seen or unseen.

Contemplation, 1915

Against Intrusion

When my friend drove up the mountain
it changed itself into a big
lump of land with lots of snow on it,
and slopes of arid scree.
Another friend climbed it the hard way:
exciting to stay the course, get to the top—
but no sense of height there, nothing to see but
generic mist and snow.
As for me,
when my photos come back developed,
there's just the lake, the south shore of the lake,
the middle distance. No mountain.
            How clearly it speaks! *Respect, perspective,
privacy,* it teaches. *Indulgence
of curiosity increases
ignorance of the essential.*
What does it serve to insist
on knowing more than that a mountain,
forbearing—so far—from volcanic rage,
blesses the city it is poised above, angelic guardian
at rest on sustaining air, and that its vanishings
are needful, as silence is to music?

Open Secret

Perhaps one day I shall let myself
approach the mountain—
hear the streams which must flow down it,
lie in a flowering meadow, even
touch my hand to the snow.
Perhaps not. I have no longing to do so.
I have visited other mountain heights.
This one is not, I think, to be known
by close scrutiny, by touch of foot or hand
or entire outstretched body; not by any
familiarity of behavior, any acquaintance
with its geology or the scarring roads
humans have carved in its flanks.
This mountain's power
lies in the open secret of its remote
apparition, silvery low-relief
coming and going moonlike at the horizon,
always loftier, lonelier, than I ever remember.

(Opposite page) Doe in fog

Steep slopes where fire has destroyed forests are more avalanche-prone than those where trees are helping to hold the snow.

Continuity and Change

Rainier's ancient heather communities have somehow escaped the seesaw of climate. Protected by snow in winter, and inherently drought-resistant in summer, their claim to the land has lasted for millennia. The Mountain's gardenlike meadows as a whole, however, ride the seesaw. Trees started an invasion in the 1930s and they noticeably stepped up their advance beginning in the 1980s. If warming continues, the trees' pace probably will quicken still more. Today's visitors stroll across a broad meadow mosaic broken by slopes newly shaggy with fir saplings. Tomorrow's visitors may find mostly trees, with flower patches here and there. Treeline rose during the warmer period that began at the end of the Ice Age, 9,000 years ago. It dropped, beginning about 5,000 years ago, as climate cooled. Now it is again rising.

Lowland forests seem more timeless than this. They close in upon themselves, do not tempt eye or mind with a distant horizon. To sit beneath giant Douglas-firs or silver firs, or to walk among redcedars, is to find the reassurance of something bigger and older than ourselves. Trunks are straight, with first branches 100 feet above the ground and total heights as great as a twenty-storey building. Diameters are four to five feet. Lives date from a time before Columbus headed west—or even twice that long ago.

WORTH FIGHTING FOR

Help Your Park Ranger PREVENT FIRES

NATIONAL PARK SERVICE · U. S. DEPARTMENT OF THE INTERIOR

Suppressing all fires is no longer considered ecologically wise.

We sense stability, but we are looking at change. Rainier's forest cloaks 200 square miles of ridges and valleys, a remnant of what once seemed endless but now—outside the park—is cut over and paved over and populated. Inside the park, the forest continuity is a mix supported by differing soils, on differing slopes and valley bottoms, exposed in differing degrees to sunlight and snowfall. In places such as the Cougar Rock Campground above Longmire, lahars have set the clock back to zero, leaving such poor soil that Douglas-firs a thousand years old may have trunks little more than two feet in diameter. In other places floods have toppled giants, or advancing glaciers have overridden them. Windstorms have left patches of broken stumps and jack-strawed logs. Avalanches have streaked slopes, breaking and ripping trees grown tall in the years since the previous avalanche, and sliding over shrubby vine maple and Sitka alder that are hunkered within the lower snowpack, supple enough to bend without snapping.

And there is fire—catastrophic fire. Water may drip, trickle, gurgle, rush, roar, and swirl gray veils of mist. Its sogginess does not preclude fire. Indian people regularly set fires to manage Rainier's high country. "That's so the berries would come back," says Puyallup tribal member Karen Reed-Squally, a basketmaker and consultant at the Washington State History Museum. "If you don't burn those sites, the trees come in. Burning was real important. Each family had its own spot, and they took care of it."

All of Mount Rainier's forests started in response to disturbance. Most now are at least 350 years old; some are 1,000 years old.

Grand Park burned in 1966, probably as a result of lightning. No major fires occurred during the park's first two decades, but after 1925 a series of dry summers set off blazes, some from lightning, some from slash fires that escaped during road construction.

Lightning starts other fires. "The land appears bleak and friendless," writes William Moir in *Forests of Mount Rainier*. "A fire has transformed the tall trees into a dismal graveyard of charred and dying skeletons. . . . In reality, the earth has just had a massage." Raindrops, previously caught by the trees' canopy and held till they evaporate, instead soak the soil. Ashes provide the "sweet balm" of fertilizing minerals. Sunlight warms the soil and evokes "dormant responses [held in check by] long centuries of cool shade. Now, with the suppressive effects of the tree layer removed, a new plant life is ready to begin." The forest is recycling.

The biggest fire yet known came in the year 1230. It devastated more than ten percent of the forest within today's park boundaries but was only one conflagration of many. Counting growth rings in today's forests back to when the trees started growing indicates the dates of the fires and gives a sense of their frequency: 1303, 1403, 1503, 1628, 1688, 1702, 1803, 1825, 1856, 1858, 1872, 1886, 1897, 1930, 1934. These are years that correlate with prolonged summer and fall droughts. The odds of wildfire at any particular spot average about once every 400 years.

If fire overtakes a slope mantled by silver fir, the heat will be intense enough to send flames racing through the forest canopy as well as along the ground. Only scattered survivors will stand; the fire's main legacy will be new openings, where bracken fern may sprout, its spores borne by wind. Once established, the fern is likely to thrive more than a century while a new forest grows up through it. Snowbrush also follows fire. Its hard-coated seeds may lie dormant for decades or even centuries until, cracked by heat, they absorb moisture and germinate. Vine maple, too, follows a survival technique. It sprouts into spindly shrubs wherever its branches touch soil or are buried.

In the western hemlock forests of valley-bottoms, a different postfire sequence takes place. Douglas-fir and perhaps noble fir and western white pine are most likely to lead the reconquest. They thrive in sunny openings and, after a century, will form a lofty green parasol shading the forest floor. Their own progeny cannot grow in such dim light, but western hemlock will sprout successfully in the moist bark furrows or rotting wood of fallen Douglas-fir. The hemlock grow into seedlings, then saplings, then rivals of the existing forest, then its ultimate successor. Some Douglas-fir may remain as a forest component for 600 years

Log of a Lookout

Sample entries from the official logs of Mount Rainier fire lookouts, 1950s

Weather:
• Rain spattering against my east and south windows. No visibility at all.
• Gave Gobblers Knob a call at 5:00 a.m. so Ron could see the sunrise, too.
• Fogged in and raining. Can't see to look for fires. Too cold to work outside. Baked a cake and read *The Abominable Snowman*.
• Lightning tonight. Am on radio standby; must call the fire dispatcher at 12 midnight and 4 a.m.

Work:
• Painted the banister and now have a collection of stuck flies. Note to the future: Paint only in shade around here unless you are an entomologist.
• Glad now that the district ranger asked me to give the trail riders a talk. Can they throw a feed! Had trouble finding them; followed wrong set of horse tracks but made it in time for dinner.
• Made a damn fool of myself by reporting a pile of gray rocks as a smoke. Called the rangers out to check it for nothing.
• 25 minutes down and back to get water at pool by bridge, *including* time spent filling waterbag.

(Right) Baking biscuits

(Below) In the 1930s, Westinghouse researchers came to Rainier to demonstrate radios as a new technology. By the 1950s, a man with a ten-pound portable radio could hope for two-way contact reaching about forty miles. A sixty-pound unit might reach sixty miles.

Using a "Merry Packer," a 1950s summer ranger and a fire guard pack food and supplies through a 1936 burn to the Sunset Lookout. The flowers are beargrass.

Wildlife:
• Watched a big beautiful hawk gliding around lookout. Should note there's a large swallow-like bird that has taken up residence here. Looks like an arctic tern to me, but must not be. There is a goat feeding on the west slopes of Mt. Wow.
• A bear walked up the steps and looked in the window from the catwalk. A yeti!

Daily Life:
• A wild day. Morning calm; then visitors like crazy, including friends from Denver who left me an orange and a half tin of deviled ham. Also had high school students who knocked Sig's biochemistry book off the catwalk. It suffered only grass stains.

• Visitors arrived just before supper, when I was trying to compose a sonnet. However, they had a good-looking daughter and left me a plastic bag of grapes.
• Can't figure out why all the good-looking college-age girls that come up to a lookout come dragging a boyfriend.
• Just as I was going to bed at 7:15 and singing "Ol' Man River" at the top of my lungs, two hikers arrived to photograph the sunset.
• Watched two parties on the Tahoma Icefall today. Wish I could have been with them.

An evening chess game by telephone links the Sunset and Gobblers Knob lookouts, fifteen miles apart by road and trail.

• Baked biscuits and ate them all (7). Mike called from Sunset and we discussed Chinese recipes for half an hour.
• Phone to Sunset Lookout has gone from good, to sporadic, to zero. Guess that stalemates our chess games for a while.

Random Thought:
• There are 10,629 steps between here and the road.

Forest complexity:
(top) Douglas-fir cone,
woodpecker holes, devil's club;
(middle) sapsucker, deer fawn;
(bottom) oxalis, tree frog

or more. Theoretically, the hemlock forest will endure until the climate changes—or the next disturbance restarts the whole process. Individual trees remain after their general forest type has surrendered. Douglas-fir 750 years old are not uncommon, and some last for 1,000 years and more. They grow slowly and live long. Individual hemlocks occasionally reach 400 to 500 years of age. The oldest known tree in the park is an Alaska yellow cedar in the Carbon River area. It is a monarch seven feet in diameter and 1,200 years old. It stands among other giant cedars, evidence of a millennium without catastrophic disturbance.

The paradox of the Mountain as a physical presence is that, though it seems constant, it is constantly changing. So too is the life upon it. In only one season's time, after part of the Paradise Ice Caves collapsed in 1928, moss and algae started to dot rock unexposed to light for centuries. After six months, a hundred square feet of raw rubble were hosting two kinds of moss, an alga, a lichen, horsetail, two grasses, and yellow monkey flower. When a tree falls in the forest, its store of nutrients and its claim to light flows back into the system. Prostrate, the tree becomes a nurse log for future forest giants. When a tree dies but still stands, it becomes a banquet table for bacteria, fungi, and beetles, and therefore for hungry woodpeckers, whose foraging results in cavities large enough to become apartments for bats, squirrels, voles, and owls. Death nurtures life. The community endures.

The Douglas-fir and hemlock forest along the Trail of the Shadows, at Longmire, has regrown since a mid-1800s fire.

PART 2

The Park

By the late 1890s enough people had stood on top of Rainier and brought back impressions that the entire populace felt an acquaintance with the big white mountain on the horizon. Even a camera had gone to the top. It belonged to Arthur Churchill Warner, who came to Puget Sound country in 1886 as a photographer for the Northern Pacific Railroad and two years later was asked to join a summit expedition. The well-known naturalist John Muir would be climbing Mount Rainier and writing about his trip. He needed photographs. Warner's equipment weighed fifty pounds—wooden camera, sturdy tripod, and 5×8-inch glass plates for negatives—a heavy load to add to his personal kit. But if he had qualms, they apparently were minor.

"Well it was this way," Warner wrote to his father. "I was already [*sic*] to go to Alaska when a man came to me and said 'We want you to go to Mt. Ranier [*sic*] with us as special artist.' At first I said I could not go . . . but when they said I must go and that I would be well paid I said 'All right' and on the morning of Aug. 8 at 3 o'clock my alarm went off. I turned over, rubbed my eyes and got up. I had everything ready and was soon on the way to the train."

Eight in all, the party traveled from Tacoma to Yelm, then continued with a "seven-cayuse" pack string. Travel was "hard work . . . over logs, stumps, cutting away trees, fording streams, climbing steep hills, etc." and Warner's horse "fell into the river and was nearly swept away." Worse, yellowjackets stung one of the horses, which bucked and set the kitchenware it was carrying to clattering loudly. "Poor Warner . . . saw the stuff flying," the youth who took care of the horses wrote, "and [he] began dancing around like a wild man, yelling: 'Stop him! Oh, my plates! my plates!' That put the rest of us to laughing and someone yelled back to him: 'To hell with your plates;

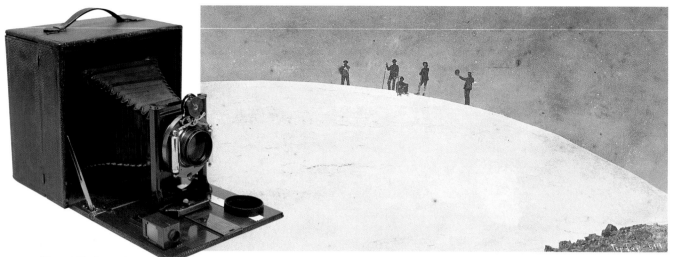

(Above) Photographer Arthur Churchill Warner in 1888 carried the first camera to the summit of Mount Rainier, a wooden model that used either glass-plate negatives or sheet film. The film, the first in the Northwest, arrived barely in time for the climb. The whole outfit plus tripod weighed over fifty pounds.

(Top right) Warner's photograph at the summit shows John Muir seated, accompanied, left to right, by: D. W. Bass, P. B. Van Trump, N. O. Booth, and E. S. Ingraham.

In 1888 John Muir and party stayed at the Kernahan homestead near Ashford en route to the Mountain. Warner photographed Muir seated under the shed roof with Mr. Kernahan to his left (with crutch) and Mrs. Kernahan by the door. Kernahan Road still exists in Ashford.

it won't hurt them.' We supposed he was worried about the tin plates but he meant his photographic plates, which he had carried so carefully all the way from Seattle."

A Century of Firsts

Warner brought back the first photographs from Rainier. The first official image, however, had been sketched in 1792 by J. Sykes, an artist with the English explorer George Vancouver. On May 7th Commander Vancouver's ships, H.M.S. *Discovery* and *Chatham,* rode at anchor in fog near today's Port Townsend, on the Olympic Peninsula. Despite the weather, Vancouver ordered three boats swung off the davits "for the purpose of becoming more intimately acquainted with the region in which we had so unex-

pectedly arrived." The men rowed, the murk lifted, and the Britishers saw "a very remarkable high, round mountain, covered with snow." The next day, with the weather "serene and pleasant," they saw it again, and Vancouver entered the name Mount Rainier in his ship's log.

The name honored Commander Peter Rainier (later full admiral), a friend from Vancouver's midshipman days. Peter Rainier's forebears had served for two centuries in the Royal Navy by the time he began his own career at age fifteen. His acclaim eventually included the capture of a privateer during the American Revolution and a non-stop ocean crossing to the East Indies, a noteworthy feat at the time. He never married, but his nephews, grand-nephews, and great-grandnephews have continued the Rainier family tradition of loyal service in the Royal Navy.

Peter Rainier, the British naval officer for whom the Mountain is named, rose to the rank of Admiral of the Blue. He gained a personal fortune in booty by capturing private ships, a custom at the time. When he died in 1808, he left the Chancellor of the Exchequer one-tenth of his wealth "for the reduction of the national debt."

English explorer Captain George Vancouver in 1792 made the first recorded sighting of the volcano he named Mount Rainier. His ship's artist made a sketch. A London artist redrew the sketch, and a third artist engraved it for publication in 1808 in Vancouver's journal.

As a young man, William Fraser Tolmie, a Hudson's Bay Company doctor, trekked from Fort Nisqually (near Olympia) to Mount Rainier to gather medicinal plants. Lahalet, headman of the Native village near the fort, accompanied him, thereby setting a precedent of guide service by Nisqually, Puyallup, Upper Cowlitz (Taidnapam), and Yakama men.

Forty-one years after that official sighting and naming of Mount Rainier, William Fraser Tolmie became the first white man to approach and record the Mountain. A young Scots doctor, newly employed by the Hudson's Bay Company in 1833, he was assigned to a post in British Columbia. En route there, he stopped at Fort Nisqually, a new pinprick of British enterprise midway between today's Tacoma and Olympia. Tolmie's arrival seemed a godsend: an employee working on a new building had gashed his foot with an axe and lay desperately ill. The wound healed so slowly that the company decided to keep the doctor at Nisqually. "His baggage is therefore unloaded and he remains here for the summer," the fort's *Journal of Occurrences* records.

Tolmie's saxifrage, named for William Tolmie

Mount Rainier, conspicuous on the horizon though fifty miles distant, drew Tolmie like a magnet. He had trained under the leading English botanist of the day, William James Hooker. At Nisqually, having no pharmacy at hand and with unknown territory to explore, Tolmie asked Lahalet, the headman of the nearby Native village, to guide him to Rainier. "I told the Indians I am going to Mt. Rainier to gather herbs of which to make medicine," Tolmie wrote in his diary, " . . . part of which is to be sent to Britain & part retained in case intermittent Fever [malaria] should visit us."

Tolmie set out on August 29th with Lahalet and four other Indian men, eager to hunt elk and mountain goats. The party returned on September 5th, warranting only a cryptic note in the *Journal of Occurrences:* "Doctor Tolmie returned safe after collecting a variety of plants." Tolmie himself wrote that he had climbed an "exuberantly verdant gully, . . . collected a vasculum of plants at the snow & . . . examined & packed them." He also described scaling a peak in the northwest corner of today's park (Mount Pleasant), from which Rainier "appeared surpassingly splendid & magnificent." He felt no compelling urge to attempt climbing the Mountain itself. His purpose was botanizing.

The first white men to climb the upper slopes of Rainier were searching for a wagon route through the Cascade Mountains, a major goal of the few settlers sharing the land with the Hudson's Bay Company. The year was 1852. The men were Robert Bailey, eventually Thurston County assessor; Sidney Ford, son of one of the first American families to settle north of the Columbia River; John Edgar, a former Hudson's Bay Company shepherd married to a Klickitat woman; and probably also Benjamin Shaw, owner of a lumber business, who had helped build the first grist mill on Puget Sound. The party spent "two days reaching their highest altitude," according to Olympia's pioneering paper, the *Columbian.* That apparently was about 14,000 feet, high enough to see the lay of the land, including "several passes at intervals through the mountains. . . . A good route could be surveyed and a road cut . . . with ease." The passes of course were not really discoveries. Indian people had been using them for generations.

By the following spring, the *Columbian* was asking for cash donations to help build the road. John Edgar returned to trace a route following the Indian trail at Naches Pass, and in October 1853 the first wheels bumped their way across the Cascade Mountains. William Tolmie, by then in charge of Fort Nisqually, greeted the newcomers. He gave them beef and told them not to settle on the hundreds of square miles grazed by the fort's sheep, cattle, and horses. The land had become American, but the Hudson's Bay Company's agricultural branch still continued its operation. James Longmire, leader of the wagon party, accepted Tolmie's direction and selected land on Yelm Prairie.

Kautz Creek, halfway between Nisqually Entrance and Longmire, is named for Lieutenant Kautz.

Historians generally credit U.S. Army Lieutenant August Valentine Kautz as the next to venture high on the Mountain. He came to Fort Steilacoom (a few miles from Fort Nisqually) shortly before the Longmire wagon train crossed the mountains. The fort had been built four years earlier to establish a clear American presence in lower Puget Sound. Kautz was called away soon after arrival, but he returned in 1857 and determined to climb Rainier. His first choice as guide may have been Leschi, a Nisqually headman tragically imprisoned at the fort for having killed white soldiers during the Indian War of 1855. At least this is the opinion of Tacoma's present-day Special Projects Engineer Bill Iyall, great-great-great-grandson of Wapowety, the man who actually served as guide. "I think Kautz wanted Leschi for the trip partly as a way to get him out of prison," Iyall says. "But it didn't work, and Leschi suggested Wapowety—although that's not how our family spells the name. It's really Opowety, without the first W."

Kautz reminisced in an 1875 issue of the *Overland Monthly* about his climb: "I was . . . young and fond of visiting unexplored sections of the country, and possessed of a very prevailing passion for going to the tops of high places." Two stalwart privates—Nicholas Dogue and William Carroll—went with Kautz and Wapowety. So did Doctor Robert Orr Craig. The men's preparation consisted of first reading about European mountaineering, then fashioning sturdy alpenstocks tipped with an iron point, and fitting shoes with an extra sole "through which were driven four-penny nails with the points broken off and the heads inside." Next, the men assembled a fifty-foot rope, "a hatchet, a thermometer, plenty of hard biscuit and dried beef such as the Indians prepare," and with that Kautz declared the expedition ready.

They were gone two weeks. Kautz, Dogue, and Dr. Craig reached the saddle between Point Success and Columbia Crest, but stopped about 400 feet short of the absolute high point. Wapowety and Private Carroll had already returned to camp. "The cleaver between the Nisqually and Kautz glaciers is named for Wapowety, so when I see it, I'm seeing my family," Iyall says.

Kautz predicted, "We are not likely to have any competitors in this attempt to explore the summit of Mount Rainier." He was wrong. Indeed, "competitors" either had already preceded him by a year or two, or climbed the same summer that he did. The date is uncertain, but the January 1917 issue of the *Washington Historical Quarterly* tells the story. It is written by Lucullus V. McWhorter, a Yakima Valley lawyer, who interviewed Yakama Chief Saluskin (not to be confused with Sluiskin, who led a later party). The chief told McWhorter of two men who rode into camp when he was young and asked for a guide to Rainier. "I look out and see them," Saluskin said. "[One had] black eyes like Indian. [The other] was "tall, slender, not good looking, but about right [with] brown, not quite red hair on upper lip.

"The old people were afraid and said: 'Do not show them the trail. They want to find money [stake a mining claim].' The Indians asked; 'Why do you go to the White Mountain?' The man said: 'We are Governor Stevens' boys. We come up the river from Walla Walla and look for reservation line made at treaty.' [1855] They had long glass to look through. Then the old people said: 'All right.' They told me to show them the trail. . . ."

After about six days Saluskin and the men, whose names are unknown, camped at Mystic Lake, on the northern flank of Rainier. Saluskin said he did not know the way from there on—"too many splits in ice"—but in the morning he watched the men "put lunch in pockets and leave camp." In the evening they returned and reported they "had gone to top of mountain and look with glass; along Cascades, towards Okanogan and British Columbia; Lake Chelan and everywhere. . . . They said ice all over top, lake in center and smoke or steam coming out all around like sweat-house. Next day I went home and did not know where these men went. I left them there."

By the 1870s, the Northern Pacific's tracks reached Tacoma and heightened national interest in the hinterlands of the West. Kautz's *Overland Monthly* article was published at this time, nearly two decades after he had climbed. A year after his article, the November 1876 *Atlantic Monthly* carried another personal account. It told of staying overnight on the summit of Rainier in 1870, saved from certain death by steam caves. Hazard Stevens, who wrote the article, was the son of Washington's first governor. With him was Philemon Beecher Van Trump, private secretary to Washington's seventh governor.

Stevens's prose was so vivid that readers felt they shared the whole adventure. A send-off party of "half a dozen carriages rattled gaily out of Olympia in the cool of the morning," escorting the climbers to Yelm and the "roomy home with a wide porch nestled among trees" where James Longmire lived. Stevens and Van Trump had called there earlier. Virinda Longmire told them her husband returned from previous trips into the Rainier country "looking as haggard as if he had just risen from a sick-bed," and she

A postcard of Philomen B. Van Trump honors his legendary role as climber, ardent park advocate, and, briefly, summer ranger. He is pictured in about 1908 at Camp Wigwam, six miles by trail from Longmire.

51

recommended strongly against a climb. So did James Longmire himself, though he finally agreed to lead the way to the base of the Mountain, where he would secure an Indian guide for the rest of the trip.

Longmire expected to find a guide along the Mashel River, near today's Eatonville, but the Indian families had been forced to move to reservations. Their homes stood empty. Just outside the Nisqually River boundary of the present park, however, Longmire found Sluiskin and his family waiting for the huckleberry season to begin. Sluiskin agreed to take over as guide.

Three days later, camped above today's Paradise Inn, Sluiskin realized that his two companions really intended to try for the summit. In Stevens's words, this led to "a solemn exhortation and warning against our rash project." Sluiskin predicted that "a bitterly cold and furious tempest will sweep you off into space like a withered leaf." Undeterred, on August 17th the two men stepped out, intending to return by nightfall. It was hard slogging. "We were now crawling along the face of a precipice almost in mid-air," Stevens wrote. Below, "a great glacier [the Nisqually] stretched away . . . all seamed or wrinkled across with countless crevasses." But finally the men reached the top. On the summit's broad dome, they took out two American flags and "waved them in triumph with three cheers." One flag had thirteen stars, the other thirty-two. Two young ladies in Olympia had made the thirteen-star flag at the last minute. They forgot about the project until the day before departure, and since it was Sunday and work of any kind on the Sabbath was a sin, they waited until midnight to take up their needles. They had time to stitch only thirteen stars, to their own design. Stevens borrowed the other flag from a friend, W. H. Cushman, who had carried it across the prairies to the California gold rush. Snapping in the wind on top of Rainier, this flag's thirty-two stars were twenty-one years and five stars outdated.

No advance notice heralded the climbers' return to Olympia, but "as the last rays of the sun . . . were falling aslant the shady streets," James Longmire's carry-all arrived in Olympia with "two bright flags attached to Alpine staffs, one projecting from each door, flutter[ing] gaily overhead." The men "were received and lionized to the full." They had gained the summit saddle nearly as late in the day as had Kautz, but unlike him, decided they "must pass the night on the summit without shelter or food." Also unlike him, they decided to press on across the broad mountaintop to its absolutely highest point, a serendipitous decision. They discovered the heat-bared crater rim, smelled its sulfur, warmed their "chilled and benumbed extremities over one of Pluto's fires," entered a "deep cavern extending into and under the ice," and spent a miserable night steam-cooking one side of their bodies while freezing the other.

Hazard Stevens climbed Mount Rainier with Philomen B. Van Trump in 1870. The two were led by Sluiskin, who probably lived on the Upper Cowlitz River. They are the first climbers with a fully documented summit success, but others most likely preceded them.

Flag carried to the summit by Stevens and Van Trump: It is twenty-four stars short of the right number.

Excitement over Stevens's and Van Trump's success was still echoing in September when two other summit aspirants arrived in Olympia: government surveyors Samuel Franklin Emmons and A. D. Wilson. They, too, asked for Longmire's help and got it, though with a warning that it really was too late in the season. Drizzle and rain beset the trip. Longmire turned back at Ohanapecosh, in the southeast corner of today's park. So did the Indian guide Muck-a-muck. Emmons and Wilson continued, gained the summit, and found it so windy they could not use their theodolite. They descended that same day and made their way east to Fort Simcoe, near Yakima. They had climbed for science, and only the few who knew they had gone paid any attention.

In the 1880s, climbers arrived at the Mountain every year or two. One party, which reached the summit from the northwest, expressed disappointment because "the view does not increase in grandeur with altitude." Another party made the first-ever climb from the east side. A third bivouacked overnight in the eastern, younger summit crater for the first time; a fourth became the first party to sleep in a tent at high camp. They pitched it on the level, pumice-covered 10,000-foot ridge already called Camp Muir because John Muir had recognized its suitability as a high camp: the presence of lightweight pumice meant the absence of wind.

In 1890, the century of discovery and exploration climaxed with one more "first," a summit climb by a woman. Fay Fuller, a teacher in Yelm, accepted a Van Trump family invitation to go with them to Rainier. Riding horses, the party reached Camp of the Clouds (today's Alta Vista, above Paradise) on the second day out. Two other groups soon arrived, including the Longmire family. Visiting the camp of these neighbors, Fay learned that a summit climb was planned and that she could go along. Consequently, as she wrote rather breathlessly in her father's Tacoma newspaper *Every Sunday*, she "donned heavy flannels, woolen hose, warm mittens and goggles, blacked my face

with charcoal to modify the sun's glare, drove long caulks and brads into my shoes, rolled two single blankets containing provisions for three days and strapped them from the shoulder under the arm to the waist, the easiest way by far to carry a pack, shouldered one of Uncle Sam's canteens, grasped my alpenstock and was resolved to climb until exhausted."

As good as her resolve, at 4:30 p.m. she and the four others reached "the tip top" and found they "could hardly stand on account of the wind. . . . We sat on the rocks and were soon damp with moisture and parboiled by the heat." In the snow cave selected for the night, Fay felt sick from exhaustion and fumes, but "after vomiting . . . felt all right and ready to enjoy the night."

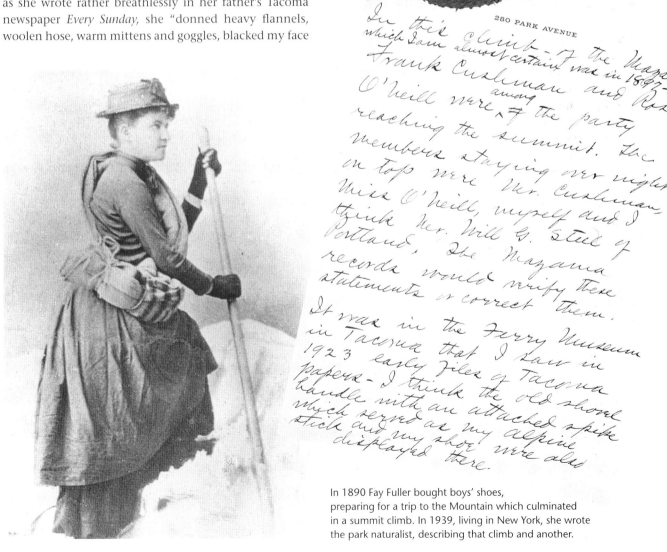

In 1890 Fay Fuller bought boys' shoes,
preparing for a trip to the Mountain which culminated
in a summit climb. In 1939, living in New York, she wrote
the park naturalist, describing that climb and another.

TACOMA, WASH. MOUNT TACOMA. *Merry Christmas to you and the rest of the family— Hattie B. Bishop.*

Printed in Germany.   Vaughan & Morrill Co., Publishers.

Tacoma boosters tried to link their city with the Mountain by urging a name change from Rainier to *Tacoma,* or *Tahoma,* apparently its most common Indian name. An early-day agent on the Tulalip Reservation gave *Dhu-hwahk* as the name, Lummi for Clear Sky—perhaps an early acknowledgement that the Mountain is not always "out."

What's in a Name?

A name controversy centered on the Mountain in the late 1800s and early 1900s. What to call it—Mount Rainier or Mount Tacoma? Primarily at issue was a Seattle-Tacoma rivalry, with business interests sometimes subtly, sometimes blatantly orchestrating events. Perhaps it also was part of the stakes in pioneering the Washington frontier. Names nurtured identity with the new land. Before the controversy ended, a Tacoma spokesman had insisted that the British Admiralty check Captain Vancouver's original log to be sure the name Rainier was present in his own, unaltered handwriting (they did, and it was), and Theodore Roosevelt had opined that Americans should not "abandon the splendid Indian name Tacoma in order to call our noblest landmark after an obscure foreigner."

The first printed mention of Mount Rainier (after publication of Vancouver's log) appeared in Theodore Winthrop's book of reminiscence, *Canoe and Saddle.* Winthrop, a Yale student, was joyfully making the Northwest frontier equivalent of a European grand tour. In 1853 he met Tolmie, at that time in charge of Fort Victoria, and through him obtained an introduction to Francis Heron, in charge at Fort Nisqually. Winthrop tells of being paddled across Puyallup Bay by Indian men en route to Nisqually and "lifting sleepy eyelids for a dreamy stare about." He saw "Mount Regnier" (the spelling used by the South African branch of the family). He considered the name "stupid nomenclature," much preferring the melodious "Siwash" name, Tacoma.

In 1868, six years after publication of Winthrop's book, a new sawmill town on Commencement Bay named itself Tacoma. Five years after that, the Northern Pacific laid its first tracks into Tacoma, followed in 1883 by completion of their cross-country railroad. The company then announced that "The Indian name Tacoma will hereafter be used in the guide books and other publications of the Northern Pacific Railroad and the Oregon Railway and Navigation Co., instead of Rainier." The coming of the railroad brought new businesses, new markets, new bustle and optimism to all communities it passed through—and Tacoma was more than a pass-through: it was the company's western terminus. When the Northern Pacific began using the name Mount Tacoma, the city did the same.

Seattle newspapers, citizens, and businesses objected to the new name and rejected it outright. Olympia sided with Seattle. Portland papers commented sometimes one way, sometimes the other. Tempers flared. Ink flowed. Tacomans insisted. And in 1890 the U.S. Board of Geographic Names met to consider the Mountain's name. They confirmed Rainier as proper, and the Northern Pacific bowed to the ruling. The city of Tacoma did not. Indeed, the city scarcely slowed its proselytizing, and in 1917 almost succeeded in getting the state legislature to pass a resolution concerning the name. Its official language pointed out that "Peter Rainier . . . never saw the mountain," and that during the American Revolution "when we were fighting for liberty, [he] was actively engaged as an enemy against us."

The House approved the measure. The Senate killed the resolution on a point of order. A second, more circumspectly worded version passed both chambers that same year and was forwarded to the Board of Geographic Names; the speaker of the house and the president of the senate were both Tacomans. The board reaffirmed its

The Name: Rainier or Tahoma?

A proper and fitting name for this great cone, and the park around it, must be officially announced, [and] once made it will be impossible to change it. It will be used in song and story; in tradition and history; poets, authors, tourists, newspapers and the scientific bodies of the world will adopt it, and it will never change. What name shall be forever perpetuated by being thus officially attached to this mountain peak? Shall it be called "Mount Rainier" or "Tacoma?" . . . What are the facts? What do honesty, euphony, simplicity, poetry, tradition, history and patriotism require of us?

Judge James Wickersham—From *Proceedings of the Tacoma Academy of Science,* February 6, 1893

The accepted right of early discoverers in a new country . . . to confer geographic names has never been reversed by geographic authority. . . . In Vancouver's application of names he was conforming to the precepts of his day and of his profession. All the names which he bestowed have been retained. Only one, "Rainier," has been questioned.

C. Hart Merriam—at the meeting of the U.S. Geographic Board with regard to the Proposal to Change the Name of Mount Rainier, May 11, 1917

Why, when General McCarver, my father-in-law [and the founder of Tacoma], laid out the first townsite over in Old Town, he came down to Portland with the plans to draft the papers. He proposed to call it "Commencement City," after the bay. I said at once that that would never do. The name was not pretty, and it was too big and ungainly; besides, it would open the way to ridicule—just think of naming a town Commencement City! Tahoma, the name of the mountain, popped into my head, and we changed the name to Tacoma. That was the way it was. This city was named in Portland, and it was named after the mountain. And Tahoma is the name of the mountain.

C. P. Ferry, "the Duke of Tacoma"—From an interview published in *Every Sunday,* as quoted at the meeting of the Tacoma Academy of Science, February 6, 1983

Aside from Dr. Cook's fanciful voyage to the North Pole, no fiction of modern times approaches that involved in the movement to change the historic name of Mount Rainier bestowed by its discoverer, Captain George Vancouver, in 1792, in accordance with time honored custom, to Mount Tacoma, on the plea that the latter was the aboriginal name. The State of Washington is thoroughly wearied with this persistent attempt to name this noble peak for publicist purposes. . . . The dignified words of the Harvard Club of Seattle express the opinion of the State as follows:

"A decent regard for history and for historical and geographical truth and integrity is of high importance in the lives of peoples and of nations. This movement, designed to subvert history and reduce this noble peak to advertising purposes, the Harvard Club of Seattle utterly condemns as unworthy, insincere and ill-advised."

—From *The Great Myth: Mount Tacoma,* Thurston County Pioneer and Historical Society, July 15, 1924

earearlier decision and somewhat acidly pointed out that the name *Rainier* had been "accepted by all the world excepting the city of Tacoma, which has ignored the decision and has persisted in using *Mount Tacoma.*"

As for what *Tacoma* means, some said "Rumbling Noise," others said "Nourishing Breast," but most agreed it means "Snow Mountain" or "White Mountain." David Denny, pioneer at Seattle's Alki Point, added that the word was generic for any peak perpetually covered with snow. William Lyman, history professor at Whitman College, reported that "a very intelligent Puyallup Indian" told him that if the second syllable of the word *Takhoma* were prolonged, the word referred to Mount Rainier; if not so prolonged, it referred to any snowy peak. George Otis Smith, director of the U.S. Geological Survey, agreed with the name *Tahoma* as generic and said an Indian person "would speak of the largest mountain in his immediate vicinity as 'the mountain,' just as the Tacoma man will today refer to 'the mountain.'" It became a bit much. As Judge James Swan, who had lived for years among Indian people and collected artifacts for the Smithsonian Institute, wrote to Tacoma Judge James Wickersham: "When a person can neither pronounce nor spell an Indian word correctly, their florid descriptions of the meaning should be taken *cum grano salis.*"

The Board of Geographic Names ruled, in effect, that it was all a fine try but the name would stay Rainier. They acknowledged Tacoma/Tahoma as aboriginal, but added that so were at least three other names and, to be consistent, "If the people of Tacoma are so eager to call places by their Indian names, why have they not adopted the unquestioned aboriginal name Shu-bah-lup, instead of Tacoma, for their own city?"

The park concessionaire touted travel by train and motor stage or by private automobile.

The park's one franchised concession, founded in 1916, used the name Rainier National Park Company, never *Mount* Rainier National Park Company.

RAINIER NATIONAL PARK

PARADISE VALLEY

NISQUALLY GLACIER

Hotels Camps and Transportation

LONGMIRE SPRINGS

RAINIER NATIONAL PARK COMPANY

OFFICERS

H. A. RHODES, President
ALEXANDER BAILLIE, Vice President
S. N. MARTIN, Secretary
J. F. HICKEY, Treasurer
T. H. MARTIN, General Manager
P. H. SCEVA, Asst Gen Manager
F. R. GRIFFITHS, Comptroller
WALTER W. FRANKLAND,
Mgr of Transportation

DIRECTORS

H. F. ALEXANDER   WILLIAM HOWARTH
ALEXANDER BAILLIE   WILLIAM P MATTHAEI
J. L. CARMAN   S. M. MORRIS
JOHN W EDDY   HARLAN I PEYTON
RAYMOND R FRAZIER   H. A. RHODES
EVERETT G. GRIGGS   A. S. STEWART
S H HEDGES   WILLIAM VIRGES
J. F. HICKEY   DAVID WHITCOMB

GENERAL OFFICE
TACOMA, WASHINGTON

The Nisqually Gate was built in time for a 1911 visit to the park by President William Howard Taft. The Secretary of the Interior, who came the previous year, had urged a distinctive marker for the entrance.

The Park is Born

A month after Hazard Stevens and Philemon Van Trump waved their flags at the summit of Mount Rainier, other mountain enthusiasts sat around a wilderness campfire in Yellowstone and discussed the wonders they had seen—erupting geysers, bubbling hot springs, great canyons, herds of buffalo and elk. Such grandeur and astonishing natural curiosities, they agreed, should be safeguarded for public enjoyment, not exploited commercially. Their campfire talk became the mythical—or at least greatly overstated—1870 moment of conception for the national park idea. Actually, the Northern Pacific Railroad backed the expedition and lobbied for the subsequent legislation. Altruism fostered the national park idea, but so did the prospect of profitable tourism.

The Nisqually Gate still marks the main entry to the park.

Two years after the fateful campfire, Yellowstone became the world's first national park. In 1890 three more national parks joined the roster, all in California: Yosemite, Sequoia, and General Grant (Kings Canyon). In 1899 Mount Rainier became the world's fifth national park. As with the others, its birth was the product of love for scenery and nature, but it was a love that wore several faces.

From the public's standpoint, aesthetics and recreation headed the list. Van Trump wrote that establishing the Mountain as a park would assure future climbers a chance to test their heroic qualities by striving to reach a goal regardless of pain. Those not fit for the summit could nonetheless revel in the camaraderie of an outing amid summer flowers and glaciers. Park advocates made no secret of their enthusiasm. Newly returned from climbing the Mountain, thirteen men and women led by Major Edward Ingraham paraded down the street in Tacoma wearing their climbing garb, dressed as mountaineers, carrying their alpenstocks, and shouting:

> We are here!
> We are here!
> Right from the top
> Of Mount Rainier!

The Northwest lifestyle had been born—and it made good newspaper copy. Why bother with Europe when splendor lay just beyond the doorstep? Why not safeguard that splendor as a national park?

Scientists, too, favored a park. To call their names is to call a roll of political power: Samuel Emmons and Israel Russell, geologists; Bailey Willis, engineer and prominent member of the Geological Society of America; W. M. Davis, Harvard physical geography professor; Major John

Revered artist and sculptor George Tsutakawa (1910–1997) was born in Seattle but lived in Japan until age 17. He found similarities between the two landscapes, which he expressed with sumi ink on rice paper. "The ink itself is very fluid," he commented in a video interview, "and the only other element to modulate the tone value is water, . . . an essential element in our Northwest scene." This view is down the Nisqually Valley with Eagle Peak to the left and conical Mount TumTum in the center.

(Opposite page) Before sunrise alpenglow, Longmire: "The Mountain is beautiful, yet treacherous," says Father John Scott, Benedictine monk at Saint Martin's College, Olympia. "And it is there even when we can't see it."

Wesley Powell, director of the Geological Survey; Bernhard Fernow, chief of the Forestry Bureau (forerunner of the federal Forest Service); Joseph LeConte, botany professor; and C. Hart Merriam, chief of the Biological Survey. Such men ensured the backing of agencies, universities, and learned societies. Many had personally climbed the Mountain. Some had made the first systematic studies of its ice, volcanism, forests, and meadows. A joint memorial to Congress from three scientific societies and two recently formed mountaineering clubs—the Sierra Club and the Appalachian Mountain Club—characterized Mount Rainier as "an arctic island in a temperate sea." On its slopes "survives a colony of arctic animals and plants which can not exist in the temperate climate of the less lofty mountains. These arctic forms are as effectually isolated as shipwrecked sailors on an island in mid-ocean." Rainier should be a national park because of its "unique interest and wonderful grandeur." It should be reserved "for the pleasure and instruction of the people."

Seattle and Tacoma businessmen and officials of the Northern Pacific Railroad also wanted a park. They saw it in terms of tourism and a widened awareness of Puget Sound enterprise. One Tacoma man wrote another, commenting that the Mountain would make "an attractive national park, tributary to our city," and he suggested a book about the park which would open and close with descriptions of Tacoma's "harbor, commerce, and scenery." The Tacoma Academy of Science printed a monograph entitled *Is It 'Tacoma' or 'Mount Rainier?'* The publication predicted: "This city will be the point to which all tourists will hereafter come on their way to examine the stupendous glaciers of this most lordly of American mountains, and it is, consequently, of great interest to our people to see to it that everything concerning this proposed park be well done—honestly, fairly and patriotically." Translation: tourist dollars belong here, not in Europe.

By the centennial of Vancouver's sighting of Rainier, proposals for a national park attracted advocates for reasons personal, scientific, and pecuniary. Timing also played a role. In 1891 Congress authorized forest reserves, the forerunners of today's national forests. The president could declare a reserve on "any public land bearing forests." The main purpose was to apply scientific forestry to the land; scenic preservation was secondary, and supporters of the reserve concept saw no conflict between using land commercially and saving its scenic value. Two years later, President Benjamin Harrison figuratively drew lines on a map and created the Pacific Forest Reserve in Washington, its name a deft sidestepping of the Mount Rainier versus Mount Tacoma issue still inflaming local politics. The relative ease of executive proclamation reserved a larger area than seemed feasible through park legislation, though the

Washington congressional delegation continued to favor a park. The reserve measured roughly forty miles square. The Mountain's summit lay within its boundaries, but the westside glaciers projected beyond them.

Cyrus Mosier, a special agent for the Department of the Interior, came west to investigate the area. He reported a wholesale stripping of the forests for two reasons. Steam power had arrived in the woods and was devastating them. Also, corporations had "stealthily crept into possession" of much of the Northwest's most valuable timberlands despite supposedly protective legislation. Mosier warned that no end seemed likely "till every tree is felled or burned and the face of the country laid bare." Logging the lower slopes and foothills of Mount Rainier threatened "to tear the frame from this grand painting against the sky."

In 1897 Congress enlarged the Pacific Forest Reserve and changed its name to Mount Rainier Forest Reserve. They also formally endorsed the use of resources such as timber and pasturage in all reserves and acknowledged the value of watershed protection, essential for irrigation needs. These land purposes were not what park advocates wanted for the Mountain. The national park idea rested on two tenets: protecting outstanding scenery for its own sake, and protecting features of scientific interest for study. A third aspect, innovative as a legal tenet, was that the beauty of the land belonged to future generations as well as to those currently alive. The Yellowstone and Yosemite legislation had defined these concepts. The Rainier legislation added a clause calling for federal ownership of all land inside the park. This affected the Northern Pacific Railroad—favorably.

The company owned substantial acreage in the embryo park and the surrounding forest reserve as a part of its original land grant agreement with the government. Aside from the overall tourism and market advantages of a national park, company interest focused on that acreage. The legislation for the park allowed the company to select public-domain land in any state it served in lieu of its Mount Rainier park and forest reserve tracts. This involved about 450,000 acres. Not surprisingly, the Northern Pacific picked lowland forests for the exchange, most of them in southwestern Oregon. As one company executive commented, the swap was gaining "property of large value in place of something of no value." Trees for glacier ice and rock. Another executive wrote: "I do not think the Northern Pacific ought to be prominent in advocating the passage of the [park] bill, but the company has friends." On March 2, 1899, President William McKinley signed the Mount Rainier National Park bill. At the time, no national park proposal succeeded without the political clout of a powerful corporate ally.

Six years earlier—in 1893—Washington Senator Watson C. Squire had introduced the first proposal for Mount Rainier as a national park. It died in committee. Tacoma papers did not even report the proceedings: they considered Squire a Seattle man. Representative William H. Doolittle introduced a similar bill in January 1894. It, too, died in committee. So did a third bill. In 1895 the two men again proposed setting aside "certain lands now known as the Pacific Forest Reserve as a public park to be known as Washington National Park." This time, Doolittle reduced the proposed park's boundaries to about eighteen miles square, half the size previously proposed. Of course it was forestlands that were removed. Doolittle also added the clause permitting the Northern Pacific's land exchange and allowing the few other private landholders in the park to make similar exchanges. This version wound slowly through committees, was passed—and pocket vetoed by President Grover Cleveland as he left office.

The final, successful bill nearly failed. Elections had replaced Squire and Doolittle with Senator John Wilson and Representative James Lewis, who shepherded the bill well. The problem was that the chairman of the House Ways and Means Committee, Illinois congressman "Uncle Joe" Cannon, did not like the whole idea and he had enormous influence with Thomas Reed, the Speaker of the House (and was himself later to become speaker). Cannon thought the park would cost more than it was worth. In introducing his first bill, Senator Squire had intimated that concessions could be "leased for hotels, stage routes, and stopping places, the proceeds of which will provide for the maintenance of the park." This struck Cannon as specious and led to a backroom discussion with John P. Hartman, a wealthy Seattle attorney who was influential in local and national politics.

Hartman grew hops near Kent, apples near Wenatchee, and wheat in Saskatchewan. He also had worked on the Union Pacific franchise and promoted irrigation and reforestation projects. He was expert in the technicalities of property exchange. Apparently he helped word the Rainier park bill's clause dealing with the elimination of private land inside the park. As he tells it, while in Washington, D.C., he arranged to meet with Uncle Joe. He found him

At first, legislation included the Mountain in a forest reserve. Congress later set it aside as a park with minimal forestlands included. (Upper right) Spray Park; (lower) Mount Rainier from the west

"ensconced in a swivel chair, with his feet on the jamb above the little fireplace where coal was burning cheerily." Cannon acknowledged he was thinking of killing the park bill and boasted that he had the power to do so. Why do it? Because "in a year or so you will be coming back here seeking money from the Treasury to improve the place, and make it possible for visitors to go there . . . and we haven't the money." Hartman promised not to request funding so long as Cannon remained in Congress, and Cannon agreed not to express objections to the speaker but to let the bill go through, "if otherwise it can travel the thorny road." It did, though with a name change. A last-minute amendment dropped Washington as the name of the park and substituted Rainier (ironically, misspelled as "Ranier").

Come all that can from near and far,
    And leave your flags unfurled;
Come view our Western Washington
    The wonder of the world.

The Swiss may boast his rugged steep,
    His glaciers broad and clear;
There never yet was mountain peak
    To rival old Rainier.
                    —*Saturday Evening Times*

Commercial logging makes virtual islands of national parks and wilderness areas. Many species become stranded. This 1992 photograph shows Rainier from west of the Glacier View Wilderness (near Ashford).

Harvey Manning: Big Mountain/Small Park.

While writing Footsore, *a hiking classic published by The Mountaineers Books (1979), Harvey Manning circled Mount Rainier musing—and muttering. The Park should be sized to fit its Mountain. . . .*

The biggest thing in my childhood sky (the moon a distant second) was The Mountain. There had to be a Park to go with it, and there was, a very big Park—immense. On fishing trips we camped in the immensity, in the deep forest which began, then, just outside Enumclaw and continued along the Model-T-size road up the White River to a dead end. The Park had been there forever, I thought, though it was actually less than a third of a century old.

A third of a century more passed, and half of another third. I climbed The Mountain by half a dozen routes, sampled the twenty-five miles of the High Orbit over the glaciers and the ninety miles of the Wonderland Trail through the meadows, meanwhile watching, year by year, the immensity of the Park shrink, shrink, shrink. The Mountain remained as high and mighty as ever but became almost pitiable, even ludicrous—head crowned, trunk and arms richly robed and bejeweled, but below the waist, tatters and rags, a green magnificence gnawed by rats—assaulted, skinned, debased. This was not The Mountain I'd known as a kid. Because The Park I *thought* I'd known wasn't. The Park was/is little, its boundaries drawn not by nature but man. Which man? Not John Muir.

Sorrow and fury (but hope, too) set me on a quest, a search for the Once and Future Park. In the twelve hundred square miles of The Mountain outside the four hundred square miles of The Park, I walked hundreds of miles, sampling a Low Orbit through the stumps, a Wonderland-Lost Trail that might yet come to be (by adding to the Park and letting a new forest grow old, giving birth to a Wonderland-Regained Trail by drawing a new line onto the map of reality.)

Even now, the Low Orbit is worth walking for its unique perspectives on The Mountain. It's known to few hikers. Most lack a taste for the stumpscapes of Hell, preferring the flower fields of Paradise and thus overcrowding the trails of the Park:

As serendipity amid the stumps, there is solitude above White River.

Atop Three Sisters, I once gazed over hundreds of out-side-Park square miles, not another human in sight among the googols of stumps—except for a chainsawyer in a pretty little grove of subalpine fir at the edge of a meadow marsh. He was making more stumps from the last of the trees in the already scalped landscape.

There's also The Divide between the Puyallup and Mashel rivers. Had it been where Senator Henry put his flying saucer (a.k.a. Paradise Visitor Center), America would come crowding to gasp at the view of The Mountain's summit icecap.

From the first, national parks have been set aside for all generations, including future generations.

Lake Louise

And for speculators in Puget Sound lowland real estate, there's the view from St. Paul Lookout northeast of Eatonville, a peaklet punctuating the awesomely wide flatlands of the Puyallup River valley. From this lookout, the mind's eye can see—and the mind's ear, hear—the spectacle of 500–600 years ago when a mass of rock and ice burst from The Mountain and swept past the peaklet, filling the valley, creating its width, and rushing on to Orting and the outskirts of Tacoma and Seattle.

Gone is The Mountain Prelude of my childhood when (Someplace out of Enumclaw) we would come to the logging frontier and the green road beyond, a narrow dirt road that led Nowhere—though construction was said to be contemplated over Naches Pass. Gone is the Prelude. Present is Stumpworld. Enduring is The Mountain. Possible is The Park, restored by re-drawn boundaries and Nature's time.

Mount Rainier became the nation's fifth national park seventeen years before the National Park Service was created. During those years, the forerunner of today's Forest Service administered Rainier. Policies slowly evolved. At first they focused on protecting flower meadows such as this, newly free of snow and lush with avalanche-lily blossoms.

Defining the Goals

On March 29, 1899, the *Daily Ledger* published an interview with Henry Carter, a well-known and popular guide at Rainier who had worked with Longmire and had then set up an independent guide service. He reported expecting "many more people to visit the mountain this year than ever before, because of the creation of the park. . . . [T]here will be an inclination to rush in and enjoy all the freedom possible before strict rules of the national park system are put in force." Actually, there *was* no national park system at the time. The army took care of Yellowstone and the three California national parks; forest reserve officials had charge of Mount Rainier. Congress did not create the National Park Service until 1916.

Park purposes had been defined for Rainier in general terms in 1899, but guidelines for implementing them had yet to evolve. A full fifteen years after the park was established, Major Ingraham, who climbed the Mountain and campaigned for the park's establishment, asked permission for 200 Campfire Girls to pick wild flowers for display at the San Francisco Exposition. "I understand that the plucking, pruning, and thinning out of flowers adds to their vigor of growth and beauty," Ingraham wrote. The Secretary of the Interior okayed the request.

First on the public's list of needed regulations was protection for the meadow at Paradise. In his *Atlantic* article about climbing the Mountain in 1870, Stevens described a fire that broke out the night before he and Van Trump left from Paradise for the summit: "After we had lain down for the night, the firs round our camp took fire and suddenly burst into a vivid conflagration. . . . The vast, dim outlines of Takhoma, the white snow-fields, the roaring [waterfall] torrent, the crackling blaze of the burning trees—was strikingly wild and picturesque."

Carelessness caused that fire. Other campers deliberately set clumps of firs ablaze as bonfires, and they cut wood freely for tent poles and cooking fires. Even the Sierra Club asked permission in 1905 to cut "trees for poles for our large tents and tables." And there were the wasps! Len Longmire, son of pioneer James Longmire, reminisced about them in the 1950s with historian Aubrey Haines. He was returning from Paradise with fresh-picked huckleberries loaded on his pack horse when yellowjackets "made a sally upon them." The horse bucked "and the berries returned to nature." Longmire reacted in the standard way: he set fire to the yellowjacket nest. The flames got away from him and burned upslope. Years later, workmen used the silvery snags from that fire for building Paradise Inn.

By "sacrilegious ax and lurid torch," a Seattle city parks landscape architect warned, the very people who admired Rainier's forests and groves were damaging them. Scenery inspired. It ennobled. Blackened forests marred the beauty. Therefore they should be controlled.

Outdoor inspiration and recreation for the public were the park's purposes. Nature should be pleasing and appealing, and park management should assure these goals. The idea of parks as wilderness preserves belonged to the future. At Mount Rainier, logging, hunting, and grazing were excluded, but mining was at first freely permitted, though it was later restricted to existing claims. The staking of new claims was prohibited. Prospectors worked properties near Longmire, in the Carbon River country, and up the White River at Glacier Basin. Some park proponents saw no problem with this. "No mineral claims need to be interfered with," wrote Fred Plummer, a Tacoma civil engineer, "as a mine, if worked, is a source of attraction to tourists rather than otherwise." Other proponents worried. The mining laws of 1872 permitted a miner to divert water for sluicing and to cut down trees for mine timbers and buildings. Abuse was possible. Was it coincidence that a stand of the park's biggest cedar trees—some of them twelve feet in diameter—was where a Carbon River company filed for a five-acre mill site? And what of another company in the same area that cut far more cedar, spruce, and hemlock than they needed for bridge construction and to corduroy muddy stretches of their access road? Or the company at Glacier Basin with a water-powered mill that could saw 10,000 board feet of timber a day? (The president of that company, Peter Starbo, ended up going to the penitentiary for defrauding stockholders by mail.)

Fires marred park lands. So did mines. In contrast, flowers and wildlife delighted the public. Early protective policies grew out of such simplistic distinctions, which were directly linked to one overarching consideration: public enjoyment. A World War I request for sheep to graze park meadows as a patriotic boost for wool and mutton production was turned down, not because their grazing would create ecological havoc but because it would interfere with human enjoyment of summer flowers. Also, the sheep might frighten wildlife just beginning to get tame enough to be easily watched. Big animals like deer, elk, bear, and mountain goats attracted attention and were

In the late 1800s and early 1900s, "magic lantern" slides of Rainier flowers and scenes enthralled audiences from Washington state to Washington, D.C. Albert Henry Barnes (1876–1920), photographer and painter, was among the most knowledgeable lecturers: he had climbed the Mountain. His magic lantern slides included hand-tinted, black-and-white photographs. From left to right: valerian, mimulus, gentian, paintbrush "good." So were "cute" animals like raccoons, squirrels, and marmots. Cougars, wolves, and varmints like fishers and wolverines were "bad" and should be eliminated. The policy held until 1931, when the director of the National Park Service listened to biologists and ruled that all wildlife should be protected, including "predatory animals [which] have a real place in nature."

Bears, in a category of their own, were both feared and sought by park visitors. Garbage from Paradise Inn was dumped into nearby open trenches and attracted hungry bears. Inn guests could pay a dollar for a ride to the "bear pits," and the sign announcing the motorcoach schedule also promised "No bear. No fare." By the mid-1930s the Park Service decided bears were not a proper sideshow. They closed the bear pits and equipped campgrounds with bearproof garbage cans and food caches. Rangers started harassing campground bears by aggressively blaring their

truck horns and sirens, flashing headlights, and doing anything else they could think of. One result was that bears learned to distinguish the ranger patrol trucks from tourists' cars.

In 1951 the Park Service circled campgrounds and Paradise Inn with electrified wire to give marauding bears a mild shock. The superintendent reported success, probably "because of the good ground contact made by the bear's big flat feet," or maybe because of their habit of sniffing, which delivers "a shock to the bear's sensitive nose." Problem bears in campgrounds or those begging for handouts along roadsides were live-trapped, driven to the park boundary, and dumped out. Usually they quickly returned to their old haunts and habits.

Park officials and the public believed that frequent blasting during road construction might be scaring animals into the back country where few visitors could see them. They

NOTICE TO BEARS
BEWARE OF SABOTAGE

We want to warn you that certain humans in this park have been passing the biscuits and soda pop to some of your brothers. Keep your self-respect—avoid them. Don't be pauperized like your uncles were last year. You remember what happened to those panhandlers, don't you?

Do you want gout, an unbalanced diet, vitamin deficiencies, or gas on the stomach? Beware of "ersatz" foodstuffs—accept only natural foods and hunt these up yourself.

These visitors mean well but they will ignore the signs. If they come too close, read this notice to them. They'll catch on after awhile.

THE COMMITTEE.

IF YOU CAN'T READ, ASK THE BEAR AT THE NEXT INTERSECTION

In the park's early years, bears were considered a source of amusement more than a possible danger or an ecological concern. But in the 1930s, the Park Service posted signs against feeding bears and developed supposedly bearproof garbage cans.

also believed—probably accurately—that trapping and poaching had cut into wildlife numbers. "Hunters line the edges of the park and butcher the unsuspecting deer" driven down by high-country snows, the park superintendent wrote in the December 1919 issue of *The Mountaineer.* Neither deer nor elk had enough protected wintering grounds. Solution? Restock dwindling populations.

Except on the Olympic Peninsula, elk in Washington verged so close to extinction that in 1905 the state legislature banned hunting them for the next twenty years. A proposal to transfer some from one national park to another seemed "eminently proper" to Governor Edward Lister, the Tacoma Elks Club, and sportsmen's clubs. Certainly they would be much easier to capture in the openness of Yellowstone than in the tangled jungles of the Olympics. Federal Biological Survey scientists objected. Rocky Mountain elk were not native, yet would breed with

remaining local elk and hybridize the gene pool. The opinion was late in coming. The first shipment of Yellowstone elk had already been released north of Mount Rainier, and two more shipments soon followed. It is assumed that some of these elk may have bred with whatever native elk remained, whether in or out of the park. In 1911 and 1912 the park superintendent had approved bringing elk from Yellowstone to Mount Rainier, but the biologists' objection stopped this. If there were to be restocking, it should be only with native Roosevelt elk from the Olympics. The whole incident generated discussion of the national parks' role in preserving nature. Was their purpose simply to provide beautiful backdrops for the flowers and wildlife that humans enjoyed, or was it to preserve samples of the environment where nature continued to follow its own course—good, bad, or cute?

Elk graze the subalpine meadows in summer. Mature bulls do not mingle with cows and young until fall, the time of the rut.

Fish did not enter the discussions. Killing them was not considered inconsistent with protecting other forms of wildlife, nor was stocking lakes and streams with species never before present seen as disruptive to the biological community. As late as 1945 the superintendent of Mount Rainier National Park wrote to the western regional director of the Park Service that taking pan-size trout from a mountain stream was the greatest sport imaginable, and "if that stream happens to run through a virgin forest, [the pleasure is enhanced]. In a national park, beside the pleasure of fishing, one gets the thrill of a day outdoors in conditions not altered by man." Protecting park resources meant confronting poachers, fighting all fires, eliminating predators, and manipulating populations to please the public.

A 1940s pack string carries bulk milk cans full of fingerling trout to be released in lakes and streams. The practice began in 1915 when 25,000 eastern brook trout—not native to Rainier—were poured into Mowich Lake. At the time, public thinking and official policy alike related fish to frypans more than to biological communities.

(Top right) Even after most fish stocking stopped in 1953, the practice continued in waters "particularly valuable for angling," according to the superintendent's annual report. In 1972, stocking stopped altogether.

(Right) Half of Rainier's fifty-one named lakes once had no fish; introducing fish has harmed native salamanders and other aquatic organisms.

The Northern Pacific ran excursion trains from Tacoma, where the company operated an elegant tourist hotel, to the Carbon River Valley. But public preference switched from that corner of the park to Paradise, which offered a better route to the summit.

Dr. Kyo Koike (1878–1947) photographed the Carbon River Valley in the painterly style. Koike was a Seattle physician who came to the United States from Japan in 1917. His work, including many Rainier photographs, was widely exhibited in the United States and abroad, and he helped to found Rainier Ginsha, a haiku society.

Getting to the Park

Soon after their tracks reached Tacoma from the Columbia River, officials of the Northern Pacific Railroad looked for a more direct route from the east across the Cascade Mountains. They sent engineer Bailey Willis to survey the foothills and canyons of the Carbon River country northwest of Rainier. He found coal and filed claims. The Northern Pacific built a thirty-two-mile branch line to Wilkeson, which was later extended to Carbonado and Fairfax. Major mines and burgeoning towns developed, and Tacoma became the West Coast's largest coaling station for steamships and an export facility that shipped coal to San Francisco.

Company interest also embraced tourism. The Northern Pacific advertised Tacoma as the logical starting point for visiting the Mountain. In 1884 it opened the Tacoma Hotel, a huge brick and stone hostelry designed by the esteemed New York architect Stanford White, from whence it offered trips to the Carbon Glacier and Spray Park. Ride the train to the end of the line at Wilkeson, then travel by horseback. What was to be seen? The glacier "entirely fill[ing] the space between two low cliffs of polished gray rock," according to Bailey Willis, writing in the Tacoma *Ledger,* and "elk, deer, and white mountain goats, . . . [their] trails like well trodden sheep paths on a New England hill," and "a curious badger-like animal [the marmot, which] greets one with a long shrill whistle that would make a school-boy envious." Grand-scale accommodations within striking distance of nature's spectacles were well calculated to keep American dollars at home.

Word of a possible second rail approach to the Mountain reached the public ten years after the Tacoma Hotel opened. Charles B. Wright, former president of the Northern Pacific and the man who selected and shaped Tacoma as its terminal city, held out one last tantalizing gift. Nearly blind and speaking from Philadelphia like a distant, age-weakened oracle, he proposed a rail line to the south side of the Mountain, where Paradise was becoming increasingly popular because it offered the easiest climbing route to the summit.

Political bickering and financial problems stalled the project. Wright died. And nothing happened until John Bagley decided on action just months after the national park was created. Born in Quebec, Bagley had started working in the Maine woods at age eleven. By the time he moved west in 1896, he was a giant of a man, both physically and as a logging, milling, and railroading baron. He saw promise in coal deposits near what later became Ashford, and also in the fifty-mile swath of timber en route there from Tacoma.

To access both commodities, Bagley and three partners bought a three-mile, makeshift, narrow-gauge railway called the Tacoma Eastern. Its past had been carrying lumber from a Tacoma sawmill down a gulch to tidewater, but, under Bagley, its future lay in punching through virgin forest from one new logging camp or sawmill to the next. In

1902 the railroad reached Eatonville; in 1903, Elbe; in 1904, Ashford. Its route passed lakes and ran along the rim of the Nisqually Canyon with its "tremendous walls of rock [and] the mad river dashing and foaming hundreds of feet below."

Bagley knew nothing about tourism, but he liked the idea of it. He contacted the Ferry Museum, forerunner of today's Washington State History Museum (and named for the nephew of the state's first governor, Elisha P. Ferry). Almost as soon as tracks reached Ashford, the museum organized a rail excursion there, then on by stage to Longmire through "an almost impenetrable forest." Paradise was only another "seven miles away and . . . well worth the exertion," according to a Tacoma Eastern leaflet. Where else could mountain lovers indulge in "picking bright-hued flowers with one hand while making snowballs with the other? . . . SEE ALL OF EUROPE IF YOU WILL— BUT SEE THE WONDERLAND OF THE CASCADES FIRST."

The Tacoma Eastern tracks are largely intact, although replaced as a travel artery by the Mountain Highway (shown here crossing above the tracks).

Michael Sean Sullivan: A Legacy Waiting

Michael Sullivan, formerly Historic Preservation Officer for the City of Tacoma, now teaches Northwest history at the University of Washington, Tacoma.

The iron rails of the century-old Tacoma Eastern Railroad still wind unbroken from tidewater on Puget Sound to Ashford, near the entrance to Mount Rainier National Park. The heyday of passenger service has long since gone, when 125,000 people a year rode the National Park Limited in the 1920s, but more than memories and ghosts remain. The old rail line is the focus of new interest in providing regular passenger service to Mount Rainier. Threatened by too many motorized vehicles, most national parks struggle to create alternative transportation systems, but Mount Rainier reaches its hundredth year with a solution in place—a legacy waiting.

The Tacoma Eastern Railroad right-of-way is publicly owned by the city of Tacoma. The line has been largely rehabilitated and, in the Elbe section, a priceless collection of steam locomotives and vintage rolling stock carries hundreds of passengers each year. At the slow pace of another era, trains can pass over the entire route from Tacoma nearly to the park, and people who have made the trip say it is *the* best way to approach the Mountain. Above Fredrickson, on the outskirts of Tacoma, the tracks cut directly and dramatically toward the Mountain. They pass along the shores of Kapowsin, Ohop, and Alder lakes and cross the Mashell River on a high radius trestle that simply takes one's breath away. The journey is marked by successive sightings of Mount Rainier, which seems to double in size after each obstructing ridge or timber grove.

The Tacoma Eastern could link the state's greatest concentration of people, in Seattle and Tacoma, with the state's greatest visitor attraction, Mount Rainier. It may soon be possible to embark at the train station on a round-trip to the Mountain, with a morning spent learning about the science, nature, and history of the region while traveling a dedicated corridor with its own perspectives on Rainier and its own rich history. Though the grass grows up through the ties in places, the iron ribbon of the Tacoma Eastern waits to be put back in use—like an heirloom handed down purposefully from one generation to the next.

1867   Mount Rainier, Washington

A 1911 Tacoma Eastern Railroad timetable for Mount Rainier purrs: "Comfortably placed in the observation car, we are started on our way full of an anticipation which cannot . . . equal the actual delights in store." This postcard apparently combines two photographs: one of a train, another of the Mountain.

(Right) In 1904, rail service reached Ashford, six miles from the park's Nisqually Entrance. "Waiting for the Train" is the caption beneath this snapshot in the Mountaineers' 1915 photo album.

The Tacoma Eastern brought 500 visitors to the park during its first year of operation as a passenger train. Ten years later, that figure was over 100,000 and the company had opened a two-storey, 36-room inn at Longmire, a "modern and artistic structure . . . on which no expense has been spared to make it comfortable and adequate. Rates including board—$2.75 to $3.00 per day." Tents squatted like square mushrooms adjacent to the inn. Nearby, James Longmire and family continued a mineral-springs resort operation.

World War I brought all U.S. railroads under government control, and when the war ended, the Tacoma Eastern's thirteen steam engines and other rolling stock emerged as part of the Chicago, Milwaukee, and St. Paul system. Rumor suggested the Milwaukee had controlled the little line's finances from the first. After the war, they worked diligently to promote The Paradise Valley Route throughout the world, boasting elegant passenger coaches and a dining car with linen and silver service. In 1904, as the Tacoma Eastern, a 9:00 a.m. train out of Tacoma arrived at Ashford by noon. In 1924, as the Chicago, Milwaukee, and St. Paul, a 7:30 a.m. train out of Seattle arrived at 10:45 and returned by 7:00 p.m.

In 1932 passenger service ended, and the year after that, the last of the old Tacoma Eastern steam engines was cut into scrap iron. The Milwaukee Road repeatedly slid toward bankruptcy, and in the late 1970s it ceased operation.

With railroads linking Puget Sound to the rest of the nation, Seattle's population leapt from 3,500 to almost 250,000 between 1880 and 1910, a seventy-fold gain, and Tacoma fairly burst with a hundred-fold gain, from 1,000 to 100,000. A young couple with a baby, living in a muddy village at the beginning of the period, would be living in a city by the time their grandchildren arrived. And they would be switching from travel by horse and train to the marvel of their own automobile. It was Mr. Ford's first Model T rolling through the far-off door of his Detroit factory in 1908 that largely determined events at Mount Rainier National Park. Cars no longer were novelties. They were *in*. Railroads had overseen the initial legislation for national parks and given access to them, but cars made the parks central in the public's affection and its recreational aspirations. Roads set the course of park development.

As early as 1893, James Longmire met in Tacoma with members of the Washington Alpine Club (immediate ancestor of The Mountaineers) and the Tacoma Academy of Science to discuss a road. His message was simple: King County was rumored to be surveying a wagon road from Seattle to Mount Rainier. Why not beat them to it by building a road from Tacoma? The tourist business would then be Pierce County's, not King County's. More than a civic gesture motivated Longmire. He was expanding his resort operation. When the county did nothing, he gathered workmen, built a semi-passable track at his end of the route, and charged a toll to travel over it. Longmire's bumpy, muddy road connected from Kernahan's Ranch near today's Ashford (where John Muir had stayed in 1888, and where there still is a road named Kernahan) to his property six miles inside the park.

Buicks en route to Paradise climb a gentle grade engineered for trotting horses, an important design consideration because the road might seem "monotonous if drivers must walk the horses far."

Upper Tipsoo Lake: Public interest in the eastern side of the Mountain came later than the interest in Longmire and Paradise. Road access followed development of the Chinook Pass link between Enumclaw and Yakima, begun in 1916 and opened in 1931.

City automobile clubs, climbing clubs, and business-men did not accept Longmire's work as the final answer to a road. They took every possible politician slithering through its mud while they crusaded for a proper road. At the same time, they also commissioned film clips to show movie-house audiences the ease of travel to the Mountain. With lively debate over whether construction outside the park should be a local or state responsibility, work on a public city-to-mountain road finally got underway. Between Ashford and the park it followed the route pioneered by James Longmire. In 1908 a Tacoma auto club measured the road's length from the Union Depot on Pacific Avenue to the park boundary at Nisqually entrance—56.1 miles—and they set out white mileage posts interspersed with a red post every five miles.

Mount Rainier National Park was the first in the country to permit cars. About sixty entered in 1907, enough to warrant establishing automotive policies. Accordingly, in 1908, the park's acting superintendent issued the first auto permit, an eight-inch-square piece of paper replete with regulations printed on the back. The permit went to Thomas Sanders of Seattle. The entrance fee was $5.00, equivalent at the time to a day's wage for a Ford Motor Company worker. It was too high and was reduced the following year. The regulations included stopping when teams of horses approached; not driving more than six miles an hour except on straight stretches; sounding the horn "at or near every bend to announce to approaching teams the proximity of an automobile"; and a final warning that violation of any rule would "subject the owner of the automobile . . . to ejectment from the reservation."

Sanders was in the vanguard of an unstoppable flood of individual drivers heading for the Mountain in their own cars, following their own itineraries. These sightseers were the public at large, not touring "customers." Viewing the park's scenery gave them a new, nationally shared

By the 1920s, park-development policies focused on serving visitors who arrived in their own automobiles. This ever-swelling tide has become impossible to accommodate by simply increasing the size of parking lots and the numbers of campsites.

experience. In 1911 President William Howard Taft rode to Paradise in a car, though it was a triumph marred by having to hitch on mules to tow the car part of the way. That year more than 10,000 people visited the park, half of them in automobiles. The next year, a car made it all the way to Paradise unaided. For a while, traffic above the Nisqually Glacier was controlled. The park superintendent's report detailed the system: "Autos leave Nisqually Glacier and Paradise on each hour, passing at Narada Falls on the half hour." Rangers in telephone contact coordinated the flow of traffic. A sign at Nisqually Glacier warned that "Boys under 21 and women" were not allowed to drive that part of the road. It was too steep and narrow and too likely to frighten them.

Work on roads at Mount Rainier was supervised from Seattle by Major Hiram Chittenden of the Army Corps of Engineers, responsible for the new grand loop road in Yellowstone. His Tacoma assistant engineer, Eugene Rick-

(Above) A windshield sticker served as the vehicle permit for 1936. By then, the park road had been built past as many waterfalls and scenic overlooks as possible, and trees blocking views were cut. "The traveler will thus be kept in a keen state of expectancy as to the new pleasures . . . at the next turn," road engineer Eugene Ricksecker had written in a 1904 report.

Early automobile permits: Even when the park road reached no farther than the Nisqually Glacier, five miles above Longmire, the combination of newly mass-produced cars and asphalt and concrete road surfaces gave birth to heady individual mobility. Today the mobility creates congestion and prompts reconsideration of train and bus service.

secker, headed the fieldwork beginning in 1903. Ricksecker's challenge was to build a road that would showcase the scenery while rising 3,000 feet with no more than a four-percent grade, manageable for "self-powered vehicles." Tourism boomed even while the road construction was underway. Hikers and climbers stayed in tent camps at Paradise and Indian Henry's Hunting Ground, another subalpine meadow reached by horse trail from Longmire. Outdoor clubs set up their own camps, some for a hundred or even two hundred people. Park visitors seeking gentility opted for the railroad company's National Park Inn at Longmire or the Longmire family's more rustic resort.

The concept of park as "pleasuring ground" held firm, though it quickly gave rise to concern over congestion aggravated by a "stub-end" road. "Through" roads would ease the problem, moving traffic through the park from one panorama or point of interest to another. Roadside trees would be cleared as needed to optimize sightseeing.

Such travel would let motorists create their own mosaic of impressions and enjoyment. It was a landscape design approach rooted in the mid-1800s carriage drives of New York's Central Park, or the paddlewheel steamboat excursions along the Hudson River. Scenery and its viewing opportunities were the underlying reason for treating park land differently from any other part of the public domain, and the expected aesthetic experience of the park was to be gained by moving through it in a motor vehicle.

Chittenden suggested a 100-mile road encircling the entire Mountain, reaching the "snout of each glacier . . . in turn." It would be one of the world's spectacular drives. Conservationists objected and it never was built, though the Wonderland Trail follows the preliminary surveys for the road and offers hikers much the same route. The road proposal and its defeat signaled a new era. How should the park's natural and cultural environments blend? Where should the balance lie between preservation and use?

Esther Macy, the park superintendent's wife, officially opens the Stevens Canyon Road, September 4, 1957. Thirty years earlier, park roads had totaled about twenty-five miles and construction of a loop around the Mountain had begun. The public, however, favored leaving the north side of the Mountain forever roadless. Work continued on the Stevens Canyon and Westside roads until interrupted by the Great Depression and World War II.

STEVENS CANYON ROAD OPENING
SEPTEMBER 4, 1957

WONDERLAND TRAIL
WHITE RIVER HIGHWAY 4.2
YAKIMA PARK 9.6 →
INDIAN BAR 5.4

dedicated
to the Memory of
EDMOND S. MEANY
1862 – 1935
President of The Mountaineers
1908 – 1935

Ever since its inception, the ninety-three-mile Wonderland Trail encircling the Mountain has attracted hikers. It was first blazed in 1915 by a party of ninety stalwart Mountaineers, plus a dozen cooks and packers.

A plaque honoring Edmond Meany, University of Washington history professor and longtime president of the Seattle Mountaineers, was set into a stone bench along the trail to Second Burroughs (above Sunrise). Dedicated soon after his death, it had to be removed owing to vandalism. The bench remains.

Paradise Inn was built in 1916. (Tents at right housed workmen.)

Building Paradise

A measure of "scenic nationalism" lay behind the entire national park concept. America had no great architectural antiquities but could instead take pride in its monumental scenery. To experience that heritage, roads and accommodations had to be built. The first five park superintendents at Rainier had backgrounds in engineering or road-building rather than natural history.

By the mid-1800s, a model for accommodations in scenic settings existed in the luxury hotels and modest cottages at Niagara Falls, the Adirondacks, and the Blue Ridge Mountains. These structures featured peeled-log construction, boulder masonry, rough finishes and textures, and massive proportions. They set a pattern for how such facilities "should" look, and it was a pattern that came west with the railroads—literally. The Northern Pacific backed construction of the huge Yellowstone hotels at Old Faithful and Canyon Rim; the Great Northern financed Many Glaciers Hotel in Glacier National Park; and the Canadian Pacific underwrote the Lake Louise Hotel in Banff National Park, Canada. The era called for combining the spectacles of nature by day with the full amenities of civilization at night and, in the words of landscape architect Frederick Law Olmsted, Jr., doing so with nothing "inharmonious [to] detract from the dignity of the scenery." At Rainier, in 1929, representatives of the four railroads serving Washington—Northern Pacific, Great Northern, Union Pacific, and Milwaukee Road—expressed enthusiasm for a joint venture backing hotels at Paradise, Yakima Park, and Spray Park. But when the company presidents met the next year, they liked the idea but rejected the plan. The stock market had crashed and the Great Depression had begun.

A postcard of Camp Wigwam shows a fifteen-tent operation near Indian Henry's Hunting Ground, begun in 1908 by James Longmire's granddaughter, Susan Hall, and her husband.

At Paradise, tourists could choose the luxury of a room at the inn or the economy of a trim tent.

Supporters of Mount Rainier felt an urgent need to increase travel to the park in the years before Congress established the National Park Service. The Forest Service had begun in 1905 and was staffed by professionally trained foresters. At their head, Gifford Pinchot actively sought to place parks and forests under single management—his. Preservationists feared he might succeed, thereby weakening the national parks' status as nature reserves. The surest way to avoid such a fate was to demonstrate clearly that parks were in use as pleasuring grounds. And the best way to draw pleasure-seekers was to offer good roads and inviting accommodations despite the fact that no well-defined agency existed to administer the parks. In 1915 Mark Daniels, the Secretary of the Interior's general super-intendent and landscape engineer for parks, summed up the conundrum in full-blown bureaucratic jargon: "[We] cannot get a sufficient appropriation at present from Congress to develop . . . plans and put them on the ground as they should be, therefore we are asking for an increase in attendance which will give us a justification for a demand upon Congress to increase the appropriations that are necessary to complete these things."

See America First! Half a million tourism dollars were going to Europe at the time. Enter the civic leaders, conservationists, and businessmen of Seattle and Tacoma. Congress established the National Park Service the year after Mark Daniels stated his case, and Stephen T. Mather instantly became its director. He knew and admired the Mountain. He had climbed it in 1905, and ten years later enjoyed a full-moon pack trip with the prominent Puget Sound men who served as a park advisory committee. Mather wanted a company to operate as the single concessionaire serving all of the park's visitor needs. His urging gave birth to the Rainier National Park Company a few months after the infant National Park Service had entered the world.

Paul Sceva, affiliated with the company for forty-six years and its second manager, wrote in his privately published autobiography about the company's origin: Numerous transportation companies competed for business to, from, and in the park and in the summer tent camps operated at Paradise and Indian Henry's. Forty-two separate operators had permits to offer services in the park. They were so disorganized "there was no depending on any of them," Sceva wrote, "[and this] caused Mr. Mather to tell a group of prominent Tacoma and Seattle businessmen that, unless they organized a company to take over all of

For seven years, Hans Fraehnke, a German carpenter, lived at Paradise Inn crafting rustic yellow cedar furnishings for the lobby. His handiwork includes handsome chairs and cedar paneling and corner posts fitted onto a commercially manufactured piano. President Harry Truman played the piano during a half-day visit to the park in 1945.

By 1917 a sojourn at the Mountain could include gourmet dining at Paradise Inn.

the [park's business], he would bring a company out from the East which would do so." The men were meeting at the Rainier Club in Seattle on March 1, 1916.

"At that time Chester Thorne, a wealthy Tacoma financier, drew up a list of what should be done and he put up $100,000 of his own money to start a program of building adequate facilities in the park and buying out the owners of the tent camps." He got others to "ante into the pot and underwrite his $100,000. They felt that this amount would be sufficient to build an Inn and provide all the required facilities."

As the secretary of the Tacoma Commercial Club put it, the contributors favored a first-class hotel "in order to entice persons of real vision and financial stature" to visit the Northwest. The Mountain would symbolize the high quality of life in the region and act as a magnet for population growth and investment. To select a site for the inn, a delegation from the new company set out for the Mountain. They reached their decision "within a few short moments—certainly not more than an hour," according to Sceva. At its upper end, the road "was not passable for transportation," so the men walked from lower Paradise Valley. When they reached the hilltop where the inn now stands, "someone asked, 'Why go farther? We can see the Mountain, see the valley and the Tatoosh Range. What more do we want? Let's build it right here.'"

Work got underway that same summer, 1916, and the inn opened the next year with thirty-seven rooms, a cavernous lobby, and a dining room that seated 400. Architect Frederick Heath of Tacoma designed the inn. He featured river-rock fireplaces at each end of the lobby and posts and rafters of peeled logs—a successful expression of public expectations for a national park hostelry. Hand-crafted rustic furniture extended the wilderness theme. Even the piano, the fourteen-foot grandfather clock, and the mail drop were clad with cedar. Tables made from cedar logs cut in half were so heavy that moving them was an eight-man job. (It still is.) Paradise Inn is a National Historic Landmark building, recognized as important to our American sense of self and place.

A flotilla of about 125 bungalow tents with two double beds, a canvas partition down the middle, "and plumbing under the bed" occupied slopes near the inn. The company assumed the public would welcome sleeping under canvas at half the price of a room, but they were not altogether right. There was demand for both. An annex quickly sprouted from the inn, two-thirds of its ninety-six rooms with private baths. At first the company opened for the summer season before July snow had been cleared from the road. They took baggage up from Longmire by sled. Guests walked or rode horses. The system was not popular. Complaints spurred the Park Service steam-shovel

The caption for this Park Company publicity photo reads: "Nature Coasting at the edge of the Paradise Glacier. . . . The participants all wear 'tin breeches,' which are furnished by the guide department." The breeches were waterproofed by ironing paraffin into the seats, a daily chore for guides.

(Left and above) Safety measures for guided trips onto glaciers included ladders and also a rope used as a hand line and for rescue. Parties as large as twenty or thirty carried only one rope, never tying into it.

(Right) In 1920, with the highway from Enumclaw approaching the northeast corner of the park, the Park Company opened a short-lived tent camp at White River. Guests could furnish their own bedding and do their own cooking, a seemingly good idea that was soon made obsolete by free public campgrounds.

crew to work harder and set company crews to clearing snow with hand shovels and army surplus dynamite. Sceva comments that one year six or seven feet of snow delayed getting the tents up until August. Then "on Labor Day they all had to come down and be stored away."

The short season meant short profits and prompted an effort to increase travel, a goal shared by Park Service and concessionaire. Eugene Ricksecker had compiled a detailed topographic map of the park while building the government road in the early 1900s, and he showed an extension past Paradise all the way to the summit. It roughly followed the route climbers used via Gibraltar Rock, astonishingly impractical as a road. Yet unquestionably it would be an attraction.

A stream of other allurements followed. In 1920, four years after formation of the Rainier National Park Company, the Tacoma *News Tribune* announced an airfield at Paradise providing daily flights from Tacoma. It never was built (though a proposed field at Longmire was announced in 1960 by Senators Magnuson and Jackson). In 1924 the company staged a motorcycle hillclimb that drew 271 bikes and hundreds of spectators. The climb's slope was so steep most of the bikes "dug themselves into the turf . . . [or] tipped over and rolled down the hill," according to Sceva. Owen A. Tomlinson, the park superintendent, wrote a three-page letter of mortification to the director of the National Park Service stating his conviction that the "vast majority" of the cyclists were interested only in the climb,

The "winter toboggan chute" at Longmire stretched for a quarter mile, "a distance ordinarily covered in 12 to 15 seconds." Park Service regulations prohibited "walking and skiing in the toboggan chute" and also stipulated that "sitting or standing on toboggans is not permitted."

Paradise Golf Course, 1930s: "[A] difficulty was that when you hit a ball off the 9th tee towards the 9th green, it just went out of sight. . . . We had to have someone down on the river flat to watch for the spot where it landed." The golf course fit the park's early role as a "pleasuring ground" and the concessionaire's need for revenue.

"not in the National Park for its scenic value." He asked the director's authorization to deny any future hillclimb requests. The scar from the one event glared as an ugly legacy for a quarter of a century. In the mid-1960s, men on the Park Service road crew carried healing soil and plants up to it and repaired the damage. "It looks pretty good now," says today's road crew foreman Chuck Heacock, who worked on the project decades ago, "but if you know where to look, you still can see it."

In another venture, the company brought a dog team down from Point Barrow "along with their sled and harness, and Dan Cakkasonoroc, their Eskimo driver." The sled's run was from Longmire, where the company had opened a hotel, to Paradise. "Dan was a loyal, fine Eskimo . . . [but he] contracted a bad cold and he retired to an Indian school in Oregon." About that same time (Sceva does not say just when), the company built a heavy sleigh and hitched up four horses to draw it for a mile or so along the road above Longmire. But, "as one lady put it, the sleigh really could have used a windshield to an advantage because there was more than snow flying as the horses zipped along." A toboggan run at Longmire was more successful. It was a thousand-foot "straight run . . . [with] a tilting platform at the top of the chute giving the toboggan a speedy start." Electric lights facilitated festive nighttime rides.

In 1921 the Mount Rainier National Park Advisory Board issued a resolution recommending a cogwheel tram from Paradise to the summit so that non-climbers could

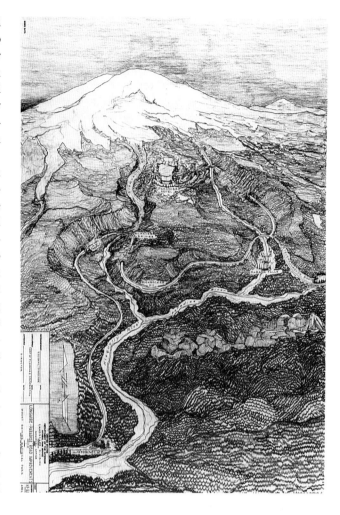

(Above) Proposals called for snowsheds to protect the road from avalanches, and for extending the road above Paradise to Alta Vista and even on to the summit via climbers' Gibraltar route. Park policies now limit all development in order to protect the natural scene.

(Left) A 1957 drawing shows a hotel proposed to replace Paradise Inn, which needed extensive repair. The public objected; the plans were dropped. The Inn, most of the park's other buildings, the roads, and the Wonderland Trail are now designated as a National Historic District because of their integrity as examples of national-park landscape design.

Ira Spring: Rainier Photographer

For decades, Ira Spring has used boot leather and a camera lens to experience mountains at home and abroad. Despite "a bit of wandering," he regards the Cascades and Olympics as his favorite ranges, and Mount Rainier as the launching ground for his career.

I remember the first time I really looked at Mount Rainier. It was 1927 and we had moved to Olympia with a view across the harbor to the Mountain. Leaving my brother and me with our grandparents, my folks rode up to Paradise for a day of sliding in the snow—the old "tin pants" method." The Mountain was clear, and I couldn't understand why I couldn't see them up there. Grandma tried to explain that it was so far away you couldn't see people, but I stayed puzzled.

About a year later Dad took us all up there. It was sunny when we left Olympia but cloudy by the time we reached Longmire, and by Paradise we were in a thick, wet fog. We passed Paradise Inn and drove to the end of the road at the tent camp on the side of Alta Vista. It was taken out later, but at the end of the thirties, when I was working at Paradise in summer as a janitor, you could still see the wreckage of the tent frames. On the way home from that first trip, we stopped at the Nisqually bridge and walked that little short stretch to the glacier. Now the Nisqually has receded far up the valley from the bridge.

In 1940 I bought my first ice axe and down sleeping bag from REI (my number is 184) and went up to Paradise in the middle of winter. I'd heard how great down bags are, so I laid mine out in the snow-covered parking lot—didn't have enough money for the Inn. Only problem was, I didn't know that the down would compress so there was nothing under me. I spent half the night trying to convince myself I was warm; spent the other half shivering.

My big break came in the summer of 1941. With a high draft number and employers desperate for help, I landed a job at Mount Rainier National Park as manager of the Paradise Inn Photo Shop. The staff was one other photographer and two salesgirls. The company wasn't sending photographers to the summit that year, but they had done so before.

Our job was to photograph the guided parties on their way to the Ice Caves. One photographer would spend the day printing pictures and the other, using a heavy 5×7 view camera on an equally heavy tripod, would take a picture of the group in front of the Guide House, run up and take more at three photogenic places along the way, and a last one at the Ice Caves.

Bob and Ira Spring's photographs have documented the Mountain—and all of the Northwest—for decades.

If there were time, he'd also make a side trip to Panorama Point and catch the horse parties. Then he'd fold up the camera, run back to the Photo Shop, develop the pictures, and have a print of each—still wet—hung on the Guide House wall when the guides brought their parties back.

Nobody had heard of instant cameras then, so seeing the pictures was more than hikers and riders could grasp. They marveled how anyone could get back fast enough to have the film developed by the time they got back themselves. Few could resist ordering. The cost was only a dollar apiece. So we'd print the pictures up and mail them out a day later.

The Photo Shop isn't there anymore. It had a showroom and a darkroom, and I slept in the basement. At the end of the season Paul Sceva, the Rainier National Park Company manager, called a meeting and said that only one division—photography—had made a profit. I intended to go back the next summer, but instead I went to the South Pacific. World War II had started.

enjoy the view. In 1947 Seattle civil engineer O. S. Willumsen resurrected the idea. He had wondered for forty years what it would be like to stand on top of the Mountain, the Seattle *Times* reported. His tram, designed with three aluminum coaches to travel partly on the surface, partly through underground tunnels, would "draw more travelers into the Pacific Northwest" than the "awesome bulk of Grand Coulee dam" and the natural grandeur of mountains and waterways combined. Willumsen expected the tram to operate 300 days a year "or more," making six daily trips to and from the summit, but, as the *Times* pointed out skeptically, "there are many miles of open highway leading to Paradise Inn which are kept open only partially" in winter. Year-round operation might not be possible.

A nine-hole golf course was "laboriously laid out" below Paradise Inn in 1931 "to accommodate the tourist who came from the East with his golf clubs." Horace Albright, director of the Park Service, supported the links,

saying: "Golf is a country game, not a city one. It can be justified in a national park easier than tennis." The play was downhill, with a bus bringing golfers back to the first tee. The second year snow "didn't melt off some of the greens until the middle of August," Sceva reports in his book. "We called it quits."

The company tried every way they could think of to publicize and promote the Mountain—and their own services. For example, Sceva told company photographers at Paradise not to hand pictures of hikes or trail rides directly to clients, but to mail them. If they received a picture while still in the park, they "might misplace it, or not get it back to their home area, where we knew they probably would call in the neighbors and friends to show them." Another publicity attempt was a "big hullabaloo in Tacoma," a parade to mark the opening of the park's summer season. Sceva arranged for a marching band and soldiers from Fort Lewis and brought in a truckload of snow so that he could "line up . . . bathing girls to ride this truck and throw snowballs at the viewing public on the sidelines." He was new to the company then and did not realize that Eastern tourists provided the profit, not local people who went to the Mountain for only a day or camped if they stayed overnight. The locals "were what we irreverently used to call 'toilet customers,'" Sceva said later. They preferred the restrooms in one of the company's inns to those provided by the Park Service, but they seldom bought anything.

Building Paradise was not easy—and not lucrative.

(Upper left) The planning team for the Sunrise development walked the ground in 1929, figuring how best to offer visitor accommodations without intruding on the scenic grandeur.

(Below) Sunrise survey crews, 1930

The summer that the road to Sunrise opened (1931), "Dancing Girls" from Miss Mary Ann Wells School in Tacoma came to be photographed.

Beyond Paradise

In October 1927, *The Saturday Evening Post* published an article criticizing the National Park Service for planning too many roads. "Why," the article asked, "should the Government incur enormous expense to encircle the wilderness with roads?" George Vanderbilt Caesar, a member of the Mountaineers, wrote the article. His remark was aimed at Mount Rainier, though couched in general terms. Parks should not be "magnets to draw in maximum tourist trade." The debate over fundamentals was on.

Mount Rainier National Park's early years coincided with rising interest in outdoor recreation. Yet the park was relatively small and, because it was close to cities, it was subject to invasion by weekend motorists. Beneath all those wheels, the surface of the park's only road—to Paradise—alternated between flying dust and bottomless mud. An expanded road system would lessen the pressure, the Park Service believed, yet a growing segment of the public wanted simply to arrive by car, and thereafter to be free of roads and commercialized activity. They did not want to find more roads. They wanted nature as is, preserved unaltered, not improved. This group definitely—and

vocally—included the Mountaineers, whose support the Park Service needed and wanted. On the other hand, the Rainier National Park Company in the past decade had invested more money in the park than had come from the federal purse in all the years since the park was created. They needed increased business to justify their investment, and the Park Service and the public needed the Park Company to supply amenities. Finding the balance was far from easy.

By 1928 Mount Rainier had become the first park in the nation to have a long-range master plan. Owen Tomlinson had been superintendent for five years. Thomas Vint directed the Service's Landscape Division—and it was landscape design that dominated the shaping of park policies. Ecological considerations had decades to wait before becoming a driving force. Three new developments were planned to take the pressure off Paradise, connect with public roads approaching the park, and boost the Park Company coffers. Hotels would be built at scenic Spray Park and Sunset Park which would be accessed by roads from Carbon River and from a new road to be built along the park's west side. Yakima Park would be developed to serve travelers from eastern Washington and to connect with the Naches Pass road (and soon also the Chinook Pass road).

Of the three plans, only those for Yakima Park were carried out, and then not as originally anticipated. This was where the Park Company and Park Service had hoped the railroad companies would finance development. Its hotel standard was to surpass Paradise Inn in size and elegance, but when the financing fell through, plans were scaled back. In 1931 a single wing of the intended hotel opened as a day lodge without guest rooms. A regiment of 215 rigidly aligned tourist cabins augmented it, along with a gas station and a campground for motorists. All were carefully situated to minimize intrusion into the environment and to leave uncluttered the sweeping view of the Mountain. Park Company brochures marketed the area as a dude ranch where "real western riders entertain and lead you on many interesting trips." The riders were rodeo contestants from the Ellensburg rodeo, which is still widely acclaimed and romanticized. Company blurbs for horseback rides renamed the long-abandoned buildings at the old Starbo copper camp, dubbing it the "Ghost Gold Mine."

Park Service buildings, constructed from 1931 to 1944, fit the frontier theme. Ernest Davidson, Vint's assistant, studied photographs of pioneer architecture at the Washington State Historical Society and decided that blockhouses filled his need. These were defensive structures built by Northwest fur traders beginning in the 1820s and by Puget Sound settlers thirty years later when Indians, resentful of losing their lands and lifeways, made scattered attacks. No hostilities had occurred at Yakima Park, which was the peaceable hunting and horseracing ground of Owhi, a prominent tribal chief who lived primarily in the Selah Valley, near Yakima.

When it came to naming the new development, Puget Sounders favored "Sunrise." The Yakima Chamber of Commerce and other eastern Washingtonians preferred "Yakima Park." To avoid another name controversy, both sides compromised by naming the place Yakima Park, but calling the development Sunrise, a confusing solution.

To the Indian people, the name remained *Me-yah-ah-Pah,* Place of the Chief.

Chief Owhi

(Below) At Sunrise, the Park Company operated a day lodge augmented by simple overnight cabins. During World War II, the company sold both the Sunrise cabins and those at Paradise to house migrant workers in the Yakima Valley and defense workers in the Puget Sound.

Dee Molenaar: Meeting the Mountain

Dee Molenaar is an artist, geologist, map maker, and former Mount Rainier climbing guide and park ranger. This account is from his unpublished autobiography, "High and Wide with a Sketchpad: Memoirs and Images of a Dinosaur Mountaineer."

1938: First Visit

It was an inauspicious spot for my brother K and me to be setting up our tent in the Paradise Campground: a small clearing in a grove of alpine fir with a camp table and stone fireplace. We had driven our '28 Model A Ford from Vancouver, British Columbia, that September day, stopping only to get a few provisions at Seattle's Pike Place Market. We'd had no view of the mountain—known to us only through enticing "See America First" travel ads in *National Geographic*—because of a pall of smoke from slash burning and the dense forest of the foothills leading to the park. Fog canceled all visibility as we staked out the heavy canvas of our tent and raised the center pole. We snuggled into our Sears Roebuck kapok-filled sleeping bags—and prayed for clearing weather by morning.

Dawn came, and shadows against the tent wall indicated sunshine outside. We pushed aside the flap expecting to face a thick wall of fir trees. But there was THE MOUNTAIN. It rose in one vast sweep from the still-shadowed depths of the Nisqually River valley below, up through steep, rocky ridges, snowfields, and glaciers, to the sunlit, icy crown of its summit.

All the visitor facilities at Paradise were boarded up for the winter. But we enjoyed a John Muir feeling of having the mountain to ourselves as we hiked the snowfields above Paradise, and on to the fire lookout cabin at Anvil Rock. One thing disappointed us, though. The pristine beauty of glistening snowfields and glaciers we'd expected was instead a brownish-gray expanse of dirt-impregnated ice and windblown dust. The mountain was not the crystal gem we'd pictured from all the travel ads.

1939: Return to Paradise

K and I returned to Paradise the following summer in early July, traveling with Los Angeles friends Ken Spangenberg and George Mayle, and this time we found snow still blanketing the meadows. Rain kept us tied to Paradise Valley, and we met Chief Guide Clark Schurman. He entertained us with tales of climbing and showed us a few mountaineering knots. He took pity on our meager climbing gear—leather jackets, knee-length boots with smooth soles (better suited to the rattlesnake

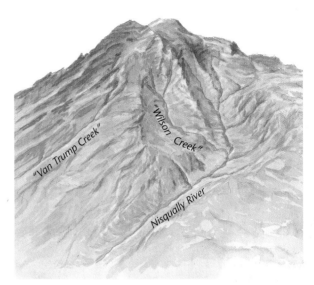

Dee Molenaar's depiction of "the Mountain undressed"

country of the Mojave Desert than to glaciers), six-point crampons, and ice axes fashioned from garden tools. We certainly had no money to hire a guide, so Schurman loaned us a couple of ice axes and alpenstocks for an unguided and unsuccessful summit attempt. We failed as much because of inexperience as because of a descending cloud cap.

We completed a three-month trip around the western U.S., then went home, and I resumed milking cows on my uncle's dairy farm a few miles from today's Disneyland. I painted a small watercolor of Mount Rainier and mailed it as a Christmas present to Clark Schurman, enclosing a note asking if he remembered "the four kids from Los Angeles in the Model-A Ford." He responded immediately with a letter asking what I was doing for a living, and what my ambitions were. When I told him I was milking cows and learning the dairy business, he suggested I could do better—go to college, study art, and guide for him during the summers.

The small watercolor sent to Clark Schurman turned out to be providential. Somehow that old scoutmaster had perceived in the painting and thank-you note a youth who would fit into his world of mountains, and he took a chance on me. It was the most important "Y" in the trail of my life—the fork that directed me away from cows and into a life devoted avocationally and professionally to the mountains. Guiding on Rainier during the summers of 1940 and 1941 started a life of mountaineering, geology, alpine art, and producing landform maps of mountainous terrain.

PART 3

The People

On September 10, 1915, the Tacoma *Daily Ledger* carried an unusual report. Rangers Leonard Rosso and Arthur White, while hiking into Yakima Park, had found about thirty Indian people "eking out an existence in the manner of their kind before the coming of the white man." They were hunting. That is scarcely synonymous with "eking," but it was against the regulations of the still fairly new national park. The hunting party's leader was Saluskin, chief of the Naches Valley Yakama and the person who, sixty years before, had guided "Governor Stevens' boys" on the first ascent of the Mountain by non-Indians. Confronted, Chief Saluskin stepped into his teepee and returned with three much-folded pieces of paper—a copy of the 1855 Walla Walla treaty and two letters testifying to his good character. Rosso and White were unsure what to do. They left and reported the matter to headquarters. Their supervisor wired Washington, D.C., and also sent Chief Ranger Thomas O'Farrell to investigate. O'Farrell found the Yakamas' camp empty.

In subsequent interviews, Saluskin commented: "You white people, you big men, I know what you are thinking, but you ought to listen to me. You were lucky to come here, but I am sorry for the way you have treated us. You now have all but a little of our land. . . . Governor Stevens was to settle all the troubles, and for this, he called the big Indians to Walla Walla in council. I was there as a boy to care for the horses of Chief Owhi."

The treaty, Saluskin knew, continued the Yakamas' right to hunt and fish and gather roots and berries "on open and unclaimed land." For generations they had been coming to Rainier. Technically, the park land had been reserved by the government and therefore was claimed. But to Saluskin, it must have looked unchanged and still available for traditional uses. Native Americans continue to feel a special tie to the Mountain. "If the government wanted to set aside land, they'd say Indian people never used it," today's Upper Cowlitz tribal member Bill Iyall comments. "Actually there was a lot of practical use of Mount Rainier—for food and for fun; for family. But the general attitude of the time was that Indians didn't live there. Reports refer to the tribal presence as 'visitors.' But Indian people *lived* there, just not all the time."

Puyallup tribal member Karen Reed-Squally agrees. "People don't have the concept of how we lived," she says. "We didn't stay in just one place, except the winter house was always the same and we'd live there the longest. But the family would split apart. The men who did the hunting would go to the Mountain, and the women who got the clams had their favorite clam beach. People today live in a house and just stay in it, but that's not how it was."

Chief Saluskin, 1915

The First People

Rainier—or Tahoma—figures in scores of myths that explain how the world became as it is and how its various aspects work together for good and evil. According to these myths, the living and non-living elements of the landscape were all people in the days before time began. They got things ready for today's world. In the myths, Tahoma is always huge, almost always female, and often a jealous wife. Typically, she has moved to her present location from the Olympics, leaving her husband (The Brothers) but carrying her son, Little Tahoma, which is the peak still sitting astride her eastside hip. Or she has come from the north, leaving both husband (Mount Baker) and children, then growing tall in her new location so that she can see back to them. Battles with other peaks, or fire and rocks thrown at her in anger by St. Helens, account for Rainier's blunt summit. She has lost her head.

All tribal groups believed that by approaching powerful myth-age places after intensive ritual preparation and prayer, a person could gain lifelong spirit knowledge. To approach without such preparation was unthinkably disrespectful and dangerous. Possibly this is what so upset Sluiskin in 1870, when he realized that Hazard Stevens and Philemon Van Trump really intended to climb to the top of the Mountain. The dirge that Stevens describes Sluiskin as singing may have in fact been a desperate apology for the forthcoming transgression. As Nisqually tribal historian Cecelia Carpenter points out in her book *Where the Waters Begin,* people ordinarily did not climb above the invisible spirit line which roughly coincided with Rainier's permanent snowline.

Below that line, people regularly relied on the Mountain's resources. "My grandmother, Hattie Allen Cross, gathered berries at Greenwater all her life," reminisces Karen Reed-Squally. "She would get out of the car with her little bucket and disappear and we wouldn't see her for hours. She'd come out at noon and eat half a piece of toast,

then go back into the woods. She wouldn't have a scratch on her hands and we'd have been massacred by the thorns. So we'd say, 'How do you do it?' And she'd always say, 'You got to sneak up on them,' and she'd make kind of a plucking motion with the fingers of both hands, a real gentle plucking motion. She passed away in 1979. Then we stopped going." These expeditions were for the sweet, low-growing blackberries that are native in the Northwest, not the riotous blackberry imports that line today's road-sides and take over vacant lots.

Huckleberries also gave Indian people reason to go to Rainier. Two dozen meadows such as those at Paradise and Yakima Park circle the Mountain, rich with berries. For the Yakama families, the lush slopes amounted to a warehouse of food different from those in their sagebrush country of eastern Washington. After they acquired horses in the mid-1700s, carrying home the largesse of the Mountain's slopes became far easier than when on foot. (The horses were introduced by the Spanish into Mexico in the 1500s and traded north). But travel on foot had long preceded travel on horseback. To follow the ripening of berries and the upslope migrations of game animals belonged to sea-sonal rhythms as surely as did the sprouting and falling of the leaves on trees, or the coming and going of the snow. People lived in autonomous groups, related through mar-

(Opposite) Lena Waters dries huckleberries the traditional way in Sawtooth Berry Fields (1936).

(Above) Yakama ladies from White Swan pick huckleberries, using family baskets (late 1960s).

(Right) Huckleberries

A prayerful, solitary quest led to discovery of a lifelong guardian spirit.

Autumn was a time to camp in the high-country in order to hunt mountain goats and pick berries. The goats were valued for meat, which was dried and stored; also for hide, horn (for making spoons), and wool (to spin and weave into blankets). Some groups hunted marmots, others did not.

riage to others. They were cosmopolitan in their knowledge of several languages and of customs other than their own. It was the 1855 government treaties that lumped Native Americans onto reservations, assigned names to them, and applied a concept of tribes.

Probably people have come to Mount Rainier for about 8,500 years, ever since glaciers melted enough to free its slopes. Archaeologists believe the early human population was small, and that people foraged the entire landscape without ties to any particular location. As population and competition increased, a need to harvest, process, and store great quantities of resources led to village life. People tethered themselves into communities, yet still proceeded to garner the entire landscape. Salmon sustained them. And so it continues. The fish fatten on the nourishing soup of the ocean, but return to the rivers flowing from Tahoma's snow and ice. In a sense, the salmon, too, garner the entire landscape.

In the high country, women picked and men hunted. Nisqually, Puyallup, and Muckleshoot women built smoldering fires and rigged simple racks with cattail and cedar-bark mats on which to dry berries. Yakama and Taidnapam women preferred long trenches with mats holding berries along one side of the trench mound, faced by a fire on the other side. Cedar bark or root containers helped keep the berries from spoiling. "If you pick the berries into cedar

baskets," Karen Reed-Squally says, "they stay fresh for two or three days. You can make temporary baskets. Just take pieces of cedar bark and fold them around and sew the opening."

At least two rock shelters on Rainier's high flanks have Yakama names that translate as 'where people dried goat meat.' Deer also were major prey, and some groups valued the fat and fur of marmots. The Yakama did not. They associated marmots with mythical Little People, "whose whistling might seduce a lone hunter, calling him ever on until he loses all track of time, space, and identity," according to what hunters told ethnologist Eugene Hunn.

Grouse made an easy addition to camp menus: the birds gorged on fermenting berries and got tipsy. Even children could catch them. Band-tailed pigeons, robins, flickers, and bluebirds also over-indulged; they had beautiful feathers, if scant flesh. Lily bulbs and springbeauty roots were easy to pry out with a digging stick. Gathering, drying, and storing medicine plants replenished pharmacies. Sharp-edged beargrass bloodied the fingers, but supplied women with a white weft for basket designs.

Gathering basket materials and medicine plants concerns Indian people today. Boundaries now slice their long-treasured geography into multiple jurisdictions, and government regulations limit their access. The land belongs to a complex public—yet it remains a single environment.

Archaeologists find widespread indication that people have used Mount Rainier's high slopes for millennia. Geologic events such as ashfalls and mudflows, however, complicate the search by covering or destroying evidence. (Below) Pumice pipe bowl found in the Fryingpan Rock Shelter

The area below Knapsack Pass, near Mowich Lake, is a typical high-country environment used by Native Americans.

Gene Wiggins, Taidnapam, looks on during an archaeological investigation near the Ohanapecosh corner of the park. Indian people today take special interest in the recovery of material from their past.

(Left) Bark peeled from yellow cedar trees could be quickly folded and laced into baskets for picking berries. Archaeologists working in the Laughingwater area near Ohanapecosh found this example in a cluster of other cedars, similarly peeled.

Archaeologists have barely begun to investigate Rainier's ridges and swales. The highest artifacts they have located are two arrowheads found on Success Divide at 7,500 feet, higher than any others known in the state. The park's oldest artifact is a point found in a Stevens Canyon roadcut. It lay above Mount St. Helens Y-tephra, dated at 3,700 years B.P., but below Rainier C-tephra, which erupted about 2,300 B.P., when the Mountain began rebuilding its summit cone. These discoveries are not definitive; they are simply the highest and the oldest.

Early people at Rainier could not have carried much with them, and the dynamic nature of Rainier's landscape further diminishes the odds of discovery. Eruptions bury evidence of human presence; mudflows and floods sweep it away. What can archaeologists hope for? Success so far includes: one stone quarry and several sites where stone was chipped into tools; charcoal and rocks cracked by fire in a hearth; the depression and charcoal of an earth oven; Alaska yellow cedar trees with patches of bark stripped off; eight rock overhangs used for shelter and to dry meat; cutting and piercing tools, which may be evidence of where people butchered prey; and projectile points of the sizes and thicknesses that would be expected for both darts and arrowheads.

Still missing is evidence of huckleberry-drying, such as post holes from drying racks, or elongated piles of fire-cracked rock and trench remnants. These have been found outside the park and probably will be found inside, too, as archaeological surveys progress. Also missing inside the park, but known nearby, are low walls of stacked rocks, used as hunting blinds or for wind protection while sleeping.

"A sense of geography and belonging to it is on people's minds today," says Bill Iyall. "Where we went for berries . . . our family's favorite hunting area . . . what medicine plants we used.

"We're tracing Indian trails onto maps now. I drove with my Uncle Archie and he'd say, 'Here's where they camped in the Ohop Valley when they went to the Mountain,' or 'The old Ohanapecosh burial ground must be somewhere around here.' My Uncle Albert carved his initials on a tree at Indian Henry's Hunting Ground, and he wants to go back up and see if they're still there.

"We're getting it down onto paper . . . where the different territories were and who our relatives are. For our family tree, we have relatives in the Nisqually, the Puyallup, and the Cowlitz; also the Yakama and the Klick-itat. They're all tied to the drainages, and so to the Mountain. The Mountain is where the drainages converge."

Elcaine Longmire traveled west by wagon with the 1853 emigrant party led by his father, James Longmire—the first wagon party to cross the Washington Cascades. Elcaine had twelve children, several of whom helped to operate the family resort business, begun in 1885. Only one building from the resort now remains, a small log cabin built by Elcaine, perhaps for use as a meathouse, perhaps as a shelter for watchmen.

Mineral Springs

No name is more associated than James Longmire's with the early development of Rainier into a park. He knew the rumpled, heavily forested country around the base of the Mountain and guided climbers en route to the summit. He climbed to the summit himself in 1883, accompanying Philemon Van Trump, who was making his second climb, and George Bayley, a California mountaineering friend of John Muir's, who at one point marveled at the swarms of no-see-ums that had turned his tea into "a nauseating puree of gnat." Longmire built the first road in the park and offered the first tourist accommodations as well as the first sightseeing trips. His grandson Leonard became the first professional summit guide. His granddaughter Susan operated a tent camp for tourists at Indian Henry's Hunting Ground. His grandson Ben became a government packer, a predator hunter, a trail-crew foreman, and a park ranger. Ben named Paradise and Mystic Lake and a host of other landscape features at Rainier—from Martha Falls, for his mother, to Devils Dream Creek, because "it is as crooked as a devil's dream."

It was by chance that James Longmire discovered the bubbling springs where he would build the family's summer home and resort business. Returning from his summit climb, Longmire searched in a fog for his hobbled horses and found them in a grassy meadow near the confluence of the Nisqually and Paradise rivers. One was drinking. Longmire tasted the water and found it "charged with minerals"—and opportunity. The public placed great faith in the healing power of mineral water. The "germ theory" was in its infancy. Mineral springs seemed as likely as any known medicine to cure disease. James Longmire claimed eighteen acres at the springs under the liberal terms of the 1872 Mining Act. He stated that the springs, which numbered close to fifty, had "mineral paint" and "auriferous gravel"—gold—and he filed a placer claim.

The Longmires promoted some of their springs for bathing, others for drinking. They provided space for camping and opened an inn. They featured rubs and massages, and they devised a "snorting pole." This wonder was an upright length of wooden pipe that tapped a sulphur spring. The fumes "took the top of your head off," according to Hollis Barnett, son of Herman Barnett, who later became the park's chief ranger. The August 9, 1890, issue of *Every Sunday,* the Tacoma newspaper published by Fay Fuller's father, carried this advertisement:

ON THE ROAD TO MOUNT TAHOMA
A WORD TO THE AFFLICTED.
AN ANTIDOTE FOR DISEASE, PREPARED
IN NATURE'S OWN LABORATORY.

LONGMIRE'S MEDICAL SPRINGS,
WITHIN EASY REACH OF OUR PEOPLE
ARE NOW OPEN FOR THE PUBLIC.

WHY GO ABROAD WHEN YOU MAY FIND NATURE'S OWN
RESTORATIVES AT YOUR VERY DOOR?
THE BEST RECOMMENDATIONS OF THE WONDERFUL
CURATIVE PROPERTIES OF THESE WATERS IS AFFORDED
BY THE CURES PERFORMED OF THOSE AFFLICTED WITH
RHEUMATIC PAINS, CATARRH, PILES AND OTHER
AFFLICTION[S] THAT HAVE BEEN PRONOUNCED
INCURABLE....

The cost for "board and treatment" was $8.00 per week. Van Trump described the scene in a letter: "Carriages, buggies, carts, wagons are sheltered under the shade of the trees and many bicycles are in evidence, many ladies in bloomers, and others in various gradations and approaches to the full blown costume. . . . The peculiar garb of the wheelman contrasts strongly with that of the ordinary mountaineer; but everyone . . . is bound for that great Mecca of tourists, the great Tahoma."

Erroll Rawson Remembers: Excerpts from an Oral History

Erroll Rawson, who was born in 1895, first visited the park in 1906. He worked there as a camp assistant in 1917 and as a guide in 1919 and 1920.

We left Seattle [in 1906] on the old *Flyer*. It was the fastest boat on Puget Sound and traveled back and forth between here and Tacoma regularly, hour in and hour out, for many years. When we arrived in Tacoma, it was just lunch time, so we went to a hotel restaurant [where] the walls were frescoed with pictures, and the tables were set with well-kept silver and linen.

Following this lunch we hurried across the city to the Tacoma-Eastern Railroad Station. There we got on the train that went up the Nisqually River valley primarily to carry logs out, but they would put on one or two passenger cars as needed for Mount Rainier, because the road from here to there was very difficult and practically impossible for automobiles—the few that existed at that time.

Going up the valley, the train clung onto the side of the walls of the canyon, partly on trestles and partly on the land. We looked down into the bottom of the gorge, where the muddy waters of the Nisqually were almost constantly evident. Ashford was the terminus of the railroad. We got off there and found waiting for us several four-horse tallyhos. People got on board above and below the luggage on the back part of each tallyho. I, being curious about everything, came back to the tallyhos late and jumped on where the luggage was, dangling my feet over the side. [Rawson was ten years old.] We were off for Long-mire Springs.

We entered the park on a modest road with the great trees around us. When we came to Nisqually River we had to ford the river. I had to pull my legs up to keep them from getting wet, because

Skunk cabbage, growing in a mineral spring, Longmire

the river was rather deep in the afternoon with the melting of the snow. It had been a warm day. . . .

Ladies' compact, a park souvenir

At Longmire Springs, boys came out from the hotel to grab our luggage and carry it in. What a fine hotel it was. It had rooms there within the hotel, but not many. But around it, with wooden walks extending out to each one, were many tents with wooden floors, and the lower side of the tent was of wood also. Mr. Gorham took one of the rooms inside, as did his daughter. But Ted and I had one of the tents together, which made it nice for us. . . .

The next day we walked the road up to the snout of the Nisqually Glacier and found that they were getting ice out of there to carry back to the hotel at Longmire. There was no electricity or other means of refrigeration at that time. They cut the ice [with axes] from the side of the glacier, where there was less dirt on it. They would clear off all the dirt and get down to where the ice was clean. . . .

The first dinner at the hotel at Longmire was a surprise to me because of its elegance. The waiters were all black and they wore uniforms. The four of us had a table together. We were offered menus by the waiters. Ted and I looked at them and were dumbfounded because the menus were in French. The waiter, who was a jolly fellow and very kindly, I remember he put his hand on my back and said: "Never mind, boys. I will bring you what you want. I know what you want." And so he did. . . .

We boys investigated the springs. There were the soda springs, the sulfur springs, and the iron springs. And there were hot springs and cold springs. You had your choice of what kind of water you wanted to drink. The springs were well kept up, not by the park, but by the Longmires themselves. . . . They had a small trail to each one. Off to one side, there were the hot springs. Two bathhouses had been set up there, well-built bathhouses. People took baths with a choice of different types of hot water. At the hotel, they would send a boy over about every hour to get a couple big bottles or jars of water for drinking. He would bring it back and put it on the clerk's desk in the hotel, refreshing it every hour or so.

tinued the resort business. In 1906, as the Tacoma Eastern Railroad was completing its elegant hotel on adjacent land leased from the government, Virinda tried to block the railroad's lease by filing for 160 acres under the Homestead Act. Eugene Ricksecker, working on the new road to Paradise, learned of her plan and immediately wrote a letter to his Corps of Engineers boss, Major Hiram Chittenden: "The matter calls for immediate action," Ricksecker urged. "No filing should be allowed within the limits of the Park. No land is under cultivation [which might validate a homestead] outside of the mineral claim. . . . All improvements in recent years, since 1903, have been made within this mineral claim and made for hotel purposes. The mining claim has not been worked in any shape or manner."

Construction of an inn by the Tacoma Eastern Railroad in 1906 brought a new level of refinement to accommodations at Mount Rainier. This photograph in the park collection is titled: "Two ladies in elegant dress."

Proposed Hotel at Longmire Springs, Mount Rainier.

A date of 1908 is penciled onto the postcard of an elaborate plan for Longmire as a major resort. Perhaps the idea originated as a railroad-company promotional dream. It seems unlikely to have come from the Longmire family, and the Park Company did not exist until later. The concept, like a world's fair layout, differs from Park Service master planning begun in the early 1920s.

Mrs. Arthur Knight of Tacoma wrote in her diary for August 14, 1893, that after three days' travel, she and her friends had "reached Longmire's and put up camp. . . . We all took a bath in the Spring and felt quite rested.

"August 15: Got up rather late and made a trip to the glacier up the Nesqualie River bed; the glacier looked like a dirty snow bank until you got close then you saw the clear ice with a cave underneath. . . . Got back to the Springs and after supper all took a bath. The water came to our necks and we were so light in the water that it took very little to support us . . . " and so on, through August 28, including mention of excursions to Eagle Peak, Paradise, and Gibraltar Rock, at 10,000 feet on the Mountain.

Park status after 1899 increased travel to Rainier. James died in 1897, but his widow, Virinda, and son, Elcaine, con-

The National Park Inn at Longmire welcomed its first guests in 1917, eleven years after the Tacoma Eastern had opened its inn. The two inns coexisted for a decade, until the Tacoma Eastern inn burned.

Virinda's attempt failed, and relations between the Longmires and government officialdom spiraled downward until the government finally bought the mineral claim in 1939. It was a sad finale to the saga of the tall and wiry pioneer whom John Muir had described as a man who "hewed his way through the woods, settled here at Yelm Prairie, raised cattle, prospected with an Indian as guide, hunted and claimed springs. He will do anything to earn money. He proclaims his good wife as a cook, and says: 'Drink at these springs and they will do you good.'"

The same year that the Tacoma Eastern opened its hotel at Longmire, Packwood pioneers John Snyder and "Water Rights" Green were scouting the forest near the southeast corner of the park. They, too, found mineral springs. Green tried to lease the land from the government but was denied. Nonetheless, he and Snyder built a trail, a cabin, and a small bath hole. In time, Ohanapecosh Camp ranked with Longmire Springs as a place to "take the waters."

Dr. Albert Wellington Bridge of Tacoma soon backed expansion of the Ohanapecosh enterprise by financing the building and operating of a lodge, cabins, and a bathhouse. An orphan, Bridge had worked sixteen-hour days for two and a half cents an hour in the Vermont woods after finishing high school. The experience led him to seek a better life, and he entered medical school. In 1909 he moved to Eatonville, Washington, where he bought an "industrial contract practice," which he extended into Tacoma and ultimately built up to a chain of fifteen clinics in sawmill towns strewn along the rail lines.

OHANAPECOSH
◄------►
HOT SPRINGS

The name Ohanapecosh is a Taidnapam word that means Standing on the Lip of a Rock. It refers to a certain rock where men stood to dipnet fish.

Local Taidnapam people visited Ohanapecosh Hot Springs long before they were "discovered" and developed. Tribal member Jim Yoke, long associated with the springs and photographed there in 1923, had his main camp at nearby La Wis Wis. According to archaeological evidence, this was a major fishing site for at least 3,600 years.

Even before Stephen Mather became director of the newly created National Park Service, the Secretary of the Interior had approved regulations requiring rangers to wear a standard uniform and to write monthly reports. This photograph dates from the early 1950s.

The practice of contract medicine grew out of the appalling need in logging camps and at mills, where injury and misery were accepted as part of the job. Employers in Washington state who contracted for medical services deducted a dollar a month from workers' paychecks. This was socialized medicine, a hot topic nationally by the time Upton Sinclair and Franklin Delano Roosevelt began stirring the political pot of the 1930s. *Time* magazine on April 23, 1934, described Dr. Bridge's clinics, which cared for "the health of some 10,000 lumbermen and miners." The article also announced that Dr. Bridge had just signed a "20-year lease on Ohanapecosh Hot Springs in Mount Rainier National Park."

Thirteen years later, a stroke forced Bridge to sell his interest in the springs, and Ohanapecosh plummeted into decline. The Park Service closed the operation in 1960. When he died, Dr. Bridge bequeathed almost a half million dollars for construction of a children's hospital in Tacoma. Renowned throughout the Puget Sound region and nationally, the hospital bears his mother's name, Mary Bridge.

Ranger Life

Twice Congress considered, but rejected, a bill for the army to administer Mount Rainier National Park. Instead, Rainier became the first park in the nation to be safeguarded by rangers. In 1903, one man took charge of the Carbon River corner of the park; another took the Longmire–Paradise district. Job qualifications soon were formalized: A park ranger should be fit, tactful, capable of handling and riding horses, and efficient with a rifle and a pistol. He also should know how to build trails and fight fires.

Allen O'Farrell, son of early 1900s chief ranger Thomas O'Farrell, described park life in an oral-history interview. The family moved from Fairfax to be nearer the northwest corner of the park and, at first, lived in a tent. Gradually they built a house around the tent, and finally they "threw the tent out the window." Allen's father wore a uniform "with a straight hat, [but] there was no office or anything like that, just a park boundary." Duties centered on patrolling for poachers and checking on miners, especially those at Glacier Basin, in the White River drainage. O'Farrell also worked with two or three men repairing and building trails. "They had one of those philosophies about building a trail. Don't build one that would go up and then go down. Just sorta go halfway around, and make the trail level. [Dad] could be a little lazy and didn't want that climb."

Through the mid-1920s, some ranger families at Longmire lived in tent cabins even in winter, and through the 1950s, the sounds of rain falling on canvas and mice marauding among groceries remained part of park life for summer seasonal rangers. Hand-cranked telephones circled the Mountain by 1929, semi-dependably linking all ranger stations, and even the world beyond, through a central switchboard at Longmire. Wires stretched from tree to tree, held by white porcelain insulators and vulnerable to falling branches and the swaying and toppling of trees during every windstorm and heavy snowfall. In his 1938 handwritten annual report, A. W. Collens, head of the park's electrical department, "respectfully" mentioned maintaining "292.8 miles of telephone lines . . . and 6 miles of primary power line. 139 miles of telephone lines were out during the winter months [and after] the snow storm Dec. 25th to Jan. 1st, 84 trees were removed from the power line and 910 trees from the telephone lines."

The Park Service shoulder patch became official in 1951. Its arrowhead shape suggests archaeology and history; the tree and bison suggest vegetation and wildlife; the mountains and lake suggest scenery and recreation. The Stetson was adopted in 1920, probably derived from a U.S. Army hat.

(Above) Park rangers, guides, and volunteers from the Mountain Rescue Council work together to rescue injured climbers and hikers. The Council was formally organized in 1948 by expert climbers belonging to the Mountaineers.

(Right) One duty of rangers was to trap bears that caused problems in campgrounds or begged for food along roadsides. Next step: they drove the trap to the park periphery and released the bear.

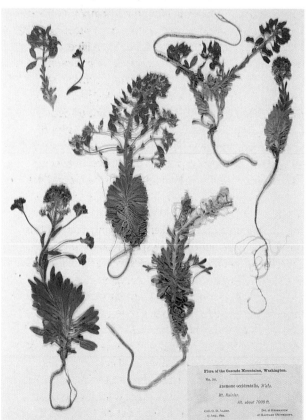

Oscar Dana Allen collected plant specimens for the Harvard herbarium in 1893, six years before Mount Rainier became a national park. His two sons, Grenville and Edward, contributed to establishing and managing the park. Edward served with the Public Land office. Grenville, the first supervisor of the adjacent forest reserve, had charge of Rainier before a separate park administration took over.

Through the 1950s, rangers helped with this maintenance, although in climbing poles and handling high-voltage wires they had only experience, not training. The ranger force no longer constituted the entire park staff, but rangers still were regarded as jacks-of-all-trades. A man newly transferred to Rainier from a desert park might be summarily sent out on ski patrol or to fight a forest fire. He learned by doing. He live-trapped nuisance bears that were bothering campers; checked the sanitary and fire-safety compliance of park hotels; packed supplies to fire lookouts; stocked lakes with fish; enforced highway regulations; led nature walks; and rescued lost, stranded, and injured climbers and hikers. Horace Albright, director of the National Park Service, once queried Superintendent Owen Tomlinson about the frequent rescue of college-age girls at Rainier, a complaint Tomlinson brushed off by saying his rangers were simply "living up to the best traditions of our Service."

Women at Rainier worked for wages as secretaries and telephone operators, but not in the "uniformed division." During World War I, Helene Wilson served as a ranger at Nisqually Entrance, replacing a man recruited by the army. Similarly, during World War II, schoolteachers Barbara Dickinson and Catherine Byrnes worked summers as

Tom Rogers: Trail Crew

The vertical wilderness of Mount Rainier awed Tom Rogers when he ventured west from the flatlands of rural Ohio in 1952. He spent fifteen summers as a trail crewman while working as a high-school music teacher and media specialist.

It was 1952. I was twenty-six years old, had finished my first two years of teaching, and had arrived at Mount Rainier to work on a trail crew for the summer. It was raining hard, and I remember asking the trails foreman, Elmer Armstrong, if the crews worked in rainy weather. He laughed and said there wouldn't be much work done in early summer if they didn't. "Trail crews are mossbacks."

We parked above Longmire and walked up the trail. It wasn't so bad in the trees because they seemed to collect a lot of the rain. Two men were bent over using tools that were new to me, something called *hoe-digs* (except there seemed to be a lot of what I took for Swedish accents, and the word came out more like *hoe-dags*). Elmer left me, and I joined in cleaning out ditches, removing branches, and clearing drain-logs along the trail. Both of the men were old-timers, drifters who had done work like this all over the Northwest, including Alaska and parts of Canada. Others on the crew called them *Uncle*—Uncle Bert, Uncle Charley.

Learning how to buck out trees that had fallen across the trail was the hardest part of the work. Some were monarchs requiring at least two cuts using saws that were five or six feet long. The old-timers were particular about their sawing partners, about how you did your part. You must NEVER push the saw away from you: only pull it toward you. They didn't like a sawing partner who tried to talk while working, either. If you kept talking after a warning, they'd stop sawing and walk away, leaving you to finish the cut alone. Occasionally we had to dynamite a tree; our saws weren't big enough to cut through them. We'd drill holes, put in dynamite, explode it, clean up the wood that came loose, then repeat the whole process.

I didn't see the Mountain all that first week or the next, even though on my days off I drove around it to White River. That side of the park was more primitive than the headquarters area. I liked it and decided to transfer there. Right away I found out that White River is higher than Longmire, so the snowpack stays on most of the trails longer. That means the White River crew is the last to get really started each summer, and *that* means we got the saws, axes, hoe-digs, shovels, rakes, peaveys, Swede hooks, winches, and sledge hammers the other crews didn't want. (Later we put up such a fuss that we got at least some tools as good as those of the other crews.)

Quite a spirit of competition developed between crews. We talked about having a relay race around the Mountain with each crew using four runners; or a contest to see which crew could get the most members on the summit on a given weekend. Nothing came of this but we did issue our own newspaper called *The Trail Crew Yell* as an offset for the park's regular publication, *The Coon Holler.* We'd write articles glorifying our own crew's exploits (most bridges built; fastest bridge built; longest bridge built; most miles covered in one day; most trees removed from the trails in one day). We'd also cast doubt on the abilities of our rivals (number of times they got lost; or did the right kind of work, but where it wasn't actually needed; or lost tools, etc.). The only thing we agreed on was making fun of seasonal rangers, who seemed mostly to sit at desks yet were full of ideas about what trail crews needed to be doing. I guess we were jealous of their uniforms.

entrance-station rangers. From that time, thirty years would pass before Rainier hired more women rangers. Much the same situation characterized the national level of the Park Service. A special committee decided in 1962 that women are "natural hostesses" and therefore might serve as guides and "rangerettes" at historic sites. The idea had actually already been tested at Rainier by the Park Company. They employed "guides, principally women . . . to conduct studies of the wild flowers and other plant life while making short walking trips from the hotel and camps in Paradise Valley."

Word of the women's effectiveness evidently had not spread. Secretary of the Interior Stewart Udall pointed out in 1967: "[It is] our concern and affection for girls that prevents our saddling them with the full load of ranger duties." Acceptance was slow in coming. The hiring of women rangers at Rainier did not begin again until 1974. Today, men and women train for, and fill, half a dozen specialities ranging from climbing, wilderness management, and law enforcement to fee collection, emergency medical coordination, and fire control (with separate specialists for wildfires and fires in buildings).

Park ranger-naturalists began filling special assignments in the 1920s, with high school biology teachers hired for summer positions. Floyd Schmoe was the first to be hired in a year-round position. He already had worked various jobs, from winter keeper at Paradise Inn, to mountain guide, to ranger. As naturalist, he received a "varmint" killed in the park—a cougar to be stuffed and mounted. He also received a pressed-flower collection, and he

Barbara Dickinson (at left) and Catherine Brynes, schoolteachers in Maple Valley, served as temporary rangers during the early 1940s. "There was great emphasis in those days on doing what you could for your country," reminisces Barbara Dickinson Hilton. "Men from the park had gone to serve in the Armed Forces, so I decided to do my part for the war effort, in addition to teaching grade school and driving a school bus." At first, WAC uniforms (Women's Army Corps) were adapted for women rangers; later uniforms had an airline-stewardess look.

Aubrey Haines: Centennial Reverie

Aubrey Haines served as fire lookout at Mount Rainier, then in Yellowstone as ranger, civil engineer, and historian. Between the appointments as engineer and historian, he returned to Rainier for five years as ranger. He is well known for his histories of Yellowstone and the Oregon Trail, and for Mountain Fever *(1962, reprinted 1999), a history of the early years at Mount Rainier.*

Looking back over two-thirds of the hundred-year period represented by this first centennial of the establishment of Mount Rainier National Park, I realize how much I owe the great mountain that loomed upon the southeastern horizon of my boyhood home. Summer employment at Rainier during the bleak years of the Great Depression allowed me to complete college and enter a career with the National Park Service, and that has been a greater satisfaction than is allowed most wage earners.

On the morning of July 18, 1934, I piled my outfit—a sleeping bag, some work clothes, and a box of groceries—on the porch of the old Carbon River ranger station, and District Ranger John L. Rickard had me sign a blank time sheet. With no more formality than that, I became a fire guard employed at $4.00 per day to watch for fires from Tolmie Peak, an outlying ridge that dominated the northwest corner of the park.

At that time, the district differed little from the wilderness of 1903 (when the Interior Department undertook administrative care of the four-year-old park). The dirt road had been extended up the Carbon River valley from the old coal-mining town of Fairfax, and the ranger station stood at the park entrance. A patrol station and a Civilian Conservation Corps camp were at Ipsut Creek, five miles above the entrance, and a small ranger station had been built at Mowich Lake. An "around the mountain" road was underway, but the lake was as far as that dream ever got—and not until after World War II.

assumed responsibility for understanding and interpreting the geology, flora, fauna, and human history of Mount Rainier. In 1925 Schmoe installed small exhibits at the Paradise Ranger Station and in the superintendent's house at Longmire. With this, he carried park interpretation a step beyond the guided walks and campfire talks the public already associated with a trip to Rainier.

From the outset, the director of the National Park Service had seen the park's mission as providing more than outdoor recreation. Learning should also be part of the experience. Stephen Mather had called national parks the "natural museums of native America." Today the park's interpretive program includes the multi-million-dollar visitor center at Paradise and a staff of naturalists and information specialists that numbers thirty to thirty-five in summer, including full-time, seasonal, and volunteer interpreters. At Longmire, a small building still displays the collection begun by Floyd Schmoe.

Among the innovative materials and exhibits produced by Floyd Schmoe, the park's first naturalist, is this "Natural History Map." It was published by the Puget Sound Academy of Sciences.

My summer home was a small wall-tent set in the shelter of shrubby subalpine firs, and my workplace was a nearby wooden stand surmounted by a tarped-over fire finder. The public did not visit that isolated place; my contact with the outside world was through a field telephone.

I helped to build the present Tolmie Lookout Station and served there in 1935 and 1936; then I was assigned to Shriner Peak, in the southeast corner of the park. The lookout there sat in a revegetated burn, in danger from lightning. Before I reported there for duty, the park fire dispatcher urged me to take the Civil Service examination for permanent park ranger, scheduled for May 27th. I did, and in due time learned that I had placed second for the State of Washington. An accompanying note commented: "Your prospects of certification favorable if vacancy occurs." The winter passed with nothing more. I graduated from the University of Washington in June of 1938, and—of course—went back to Mount Rainier for another summer on Shriner Peak.

In midsummer, Harold Hall called me from the Ohanapecosh Ranger Station. A government letter had arrived for me. Did I want it read over the phone or held until the packer could come up? I said, "Read it!" It was from the superintendent of Hawaii National Park, wanting to know if I was interested in a ranger position at $1860 per annum. In a dither over that wonderful prospect, I called Chief Ranger Al Rose at Longmire for advice, and he got Superintendent Owen A. Tomlinson on the wire.

Tomlinson said: "Don't take it. There will be something better." Sure enough, an offer from Yellowstone came along in late August, and that time Tomlinson said: "Take it." I did, and the career that opened to me sixty years ago has been very, very satisfying.

In the 1890s, when Mount Rainier National Park was new, visitors numbered between two and three hundred people a year. In 1995, that figure stood at over two million—a ten-thousandfold increase. What of the people behind the statistics? John Madden, a 1990s park ranger at Paradise, says: "Only the clothing is different—fuchsia pants and a technicolor jacket. And instead of a compass, some carry a GPS ('global positioning system,' a handheld receiver that uses signals from satellites to determine position to within several feet). Or they carry a rechargeable flashlight, forgetting there's no way to charge it. Or a cell phone, expecting a connection and a thirty-minute wait till help arrives. But people come for the same reason they always have: once they see Rainier, it pulls them like a magnet."

Outside the "blockhouse" visitor center at Sunrise, a summer ranger–naturalist sets out to lead a guided nature walk.

The CCC and the Soldiers

During the Great Depression years, from 1933 to 1941, Rainier was home to eight Civilian Conservation Corps camps of up to 200 men. Each man earned $30 a month, plus board and room. They repaired trails, cleaned roadsides, strung telephone lines, installed river flood-control cribbing, attempted insect and plant disease control, and built everything from campground tables and fireplaces to backcountry patrol cabins and fire lookouts. Nationwide, almost fourteen million people were unemployed. One working-age man in four had no job—and no hope. A million hobos rode the rails and called at housewives' back doors to ask for a meal. A thousand families a day were losing their homes.

Franklin Roosevelt, newly elected to the presidency, urged congress to establish the Civilian Conservation Corps as a voluntary program. It would give young men a chance to regain dignity and send money home while working on thousands of long-neglected outdoor conservation projects. Enrollees in western Washington assembled at Fort Lewis, near Tacoma, and on May 15, 1933, the initial group of corpsmen started for the Mountain. They were the first of hundreds to roll slowly to Longmire and the park's outlying camps.

In 1937 Superintendent William S. Nowlin of the camp at Ohanapecosh wrote to his friend, Washington Representative Charles H. Leavy, who read the letter into the Congressional Record: "All week these CCC Arkansas

Ranging from trails to bridges to buildings, hundreds of construction projects in the park came from the CCC program of the 1930s. The eight CCC camps at Rainier attracted tourists, and the Park Service regarded the men as new kinds of visitors who could build their characters while improving the park. This photograph shows work on the Klickitat Bridge.

(Opposite page) CCC men took pride in their work, and in sending money home to their families.

boys have worked out in the woods," Nowlin wrote. "They put on those Army rainproof clothes—tin pants they call 'em. They lean them up against a stump, climb up on the top and jump into them. . . . One of my 'gang' (a little fellow weighing about 100 pounds) came out to work the other day without his 'tin pants' and I sent him back to get them. There was only one pair left—size 44. Well, he got into them, bent the bottoms up so that he could walk, found a piece of half-inch rope, made a gallus to hold them up, and on the way back he gathered moss enough to fill them out around the waist. . . .

"One day we will be planting delicate, lacy ferns . . . the next we will be digging with a steam shovel or using a 'Cherry picker' to replace weathered boulders, weighing about a ton, to keep these dumb campers from driving where they are not supposed to. We build huge log tables, so heavy the people can't move them around, and stone fireplaces, and stencil and carve and burn signs on the face of a cedar log cut in half . . . and, believe me, these boys are workers. . . . I hope they make the CCC permanent, even if they have to discontinue the Army and Navy. . . ."

The Civilian Conservation Corps ended as World War II began. In place of young men who needed work, Rainier hosted soldier-skiers who needed training. Russia's invasion of Finland in the winter of 1939–40 caught the attention of military strategists. Russians had assumed that if they raised their voices, "the Finns would put up their hands and surrender," as Nikita Krushchev once summarized events. Not so. The Finns fought on skis. They wore

Today's volunteer Student Conservation Association works in national parks and forests throughout the country. Building the Nickel Creek trail shelter was one of its projects at Rainier in 1969.

bed-sheet coveralls as camouflage, attacked during blizzards, and held off Russian tanks for 105 days, though they were outnumbered forty-two to one.

During that time, ski patrolmen at Manchester, Vermont, sat one evening drinking beer and cheering the Finns. Tensions obviously were going to erupt soon in Europe; what if they spilled over and foreign troops attacked New England? Shouldn't the United States Army include a ski unit? The National Ski Association suggested the idea to the U.S. War Department. They were brushed off, but followed through nonetheless by persuading the National Ski Patrol to volunteer their services. The British army had welcomed patrolmen, and in Scotland, skiers were carrying supplies to snowbound anti-aircraft stations. Minot Dole, who spearheaded formation of the Ski Patrol, contacted former Yale classmates, who contacted General George Marshall. A few months later, the Winter Warfare Board approved standards for equipping and training U.S. ski troops.

Yellowstone seemed the best place for a base. It had snow and housing. It formerly had been a ward of the army. But Yellowstone also had trumpeter swans. Hunting had almost exterminated the species; winter disturbance now might ring the death knell. The army surrendered to the birds.

What about Mount Rainier? It was close to Fort Lewis, had adequate quarters to feed and house troops, and offered a range of winter terrain and weather conditions. Paradise too mild? Ski higher. The vertical-zones, arctic-island metaphor that made Rainier worthy as a national park could also serve national security. In November 1940, a Military Ski Patrol from the 15th Infantry arrived

In the 1940s, U.S. Army ski troops trained at Paradise, then a nationally recognized ski area. Logging, mining, and grazing profiteers had made inroads into several national parks during World War I; the Rainier superintendent had refused a request to graze 50,000 sheep but permitted 1,000 cattle at Yakima Park and Cowlitz Divide. To avoid "patriotic" contributions of that sort during World War II, parks welcomed soldiers for rest and recreation, and, at Rainier, also for infantry training.

(Below) Paradise Inn blanketed by March snow

Symbol of tragedy: The tip of the U.S. Marine plane's propeller eventually emerged from the ice of the South Tahoma Glacier.

for a half-day of "preliminary instruction excercise." Success led to a full winter of training for twenty-four ski-mounted soldiers detached from the 41st Infantry Division. They stayed at Longmire, but skied daily to Paradise. Park rangers helped to train them. The following winter, a thousand-man ski regiment designated as the 87th Mountain Infantry formed at Fort Lewis. East Coast ski clubs and college ski teams sent recruits; European immigrants and exiles volunteered; so did Park Service and U.S. Forest Service rangers.

In December 1941, the United States declared war in Europe and the Pacific. Throughout that winter, the army rented Paradise Lodge and an adjacent building from the Rainier National Park Company (providing a much needed boost for company finances). Soldiers climbed to Rainier's summit to test clothing from the army's development division. They performed sentry duty wearing sleeping bags equipped with legs and feet. They skied completely around the Mountain, ninety miles, carrying rifles and 85-pound packs.

The public still came on the weekends; Paradise was the biggest ski resort in the Northwest and was nationally renowned. The troops helped to set ski courses, furnished doctors and first aid, and handled radio communication in addition to participating in races and jumps. At a 1998 ski-troop reunion in Seattle, Sherman Smith spoke of those weekends as his most cherished memory of Paradise half a century earlier. He remembered a rope fire-escape that facilitated second-storey entry into the inn. He also remembered successfully switching large quantities of ice cream from the inn to the lodge, so that he could "build up strength" for the next weekend. He needed the strength to carry a full case of beer to Camp Muir, at 10,000 feet, where he was to help officiate at the starting point of a race. Alas, he arrived with all except one bottle broken.

The troops' rollicking weekends offset their tough weekdays. Then came spring 1942, and the 87th Mountain Infantry transferred to Camp Hale, Colorado, where they merged into the 10th Mountain Infantry Division. They fought in Italy: three months of combat brought four thousand casualties among seven thousand men. Training at Paradise must have seemed very long ago and very far away.

For thirty-two U.S. Marines and their families, Mount Rainier meant tragedy. During the stormy night of December 10, 1946, the marines' C-46 transport plane crashed into the Mountain while flying from San Diego to Sand Point Naval Air Station in Seattle. All on board died. Military and civilian pilots sought the wreckage. (During one of these searches, the pilot reported darting, saucerlike objects above the Tatoosh Range—the first UFO sighting.) Rangers and climbers from Seattle and Tacoma sought the crash site on the ground. People brought search dogs and "divining rods" to the park and offered their services. And finally, in July, Assistant Chief Ranger Bill Butler found the plane. From the Success Cleaver, he spotted wreckage on the ice below. The next day, rangers and Park Company guides hiked there, but found only parts of the plane's tail section projecting from a crevasse wall. A month later, Butler—still searching—found the main wreckage at 10,000 feet on the South Tahoma Glacier. Rangers and guides climbed to this second site, joined by military personnel. Dee Molenaar, at that time a guide, remembers that the navy men wore government-issue, smooth-soled oxfords. Fog shrouded the scene, rocks hurtled from the glacier headwall, and the ill-shod sailors slipped perilously. Rather than add more lives to the toll, the colonel from the army's Mountain and Cold-Weather Training Command, called a halt. The headwall became a headstone.

Early Outings

Soon after their parents' wagons finished rolling over and around the mountains, Northwesterners started heading joyfully upward on foot. The 1891 trek of four stalwarts from Enumclaw illustrates the point. The town had a population of 125 at the time but aspired to a substantial increase. They thought newspaper coverage might help: banners waving at the top of Mount Rainier might catch editors' attention. Oscar Brown, a major landowner in Enumclaw and later a park ranger, led the men via the Bailey Willis Trail from near the northwest corner of today's park to Nisqually at the southwest corner, a distance of about forty miles. (The route is now out of use and out of mind, though Harvey Manning, the author with Ira Spring of the Mountaineers *100 Hikes* book series, urges its res-urrection. The Bailey Willis Trail was the first lengthy one into the Rainier country, other than the routes of Native Americans. It brought the Mountain its first sightseer-tourists. Manning dreams of taking archaeologists to one of the Willis's old camps "to excavate rusted-out frying pans and broken crockery and violet-hued glass from beneath a century's accumulation of duff.")

The 1891 Enumclaw party went from Nisqually to the summit of Rainier, carrying a camera and a twenty-three-foot flagpole cut at Paradise from a yellow cedar tree. On the tall pole, they raised a U.S. flag presented by the men of their town, and a pennant the women had embroidered with the word "Enumclaw." Photographs documented the triumph. But apparently no one in the surrounding countryside saw the banners.

Asahel Curtis (right) joins Owen Tomlinson in a field discussion. The two men probably influenced the first half century of the park's development more than did anyone else. Tomlinson served as superintendent at Mount Rainier from 1923 to 1941; and, beginning with the 1905 joint expedition of four outing clubs, Curtis became Rainier's greatest advocate and activist.

Gertrude Metcalfe: The Rainier Climb (1905)

Gertrude Metcalfe was historian for the Mazamas. This note on a trip with the Sierra Club, Appalachian Mountain Club, and the American Alpine Club was published in Mazama, *vol. 2, no. 4 (Dec.) 1905.*

It is not easy to count heads on a mountain-side, where even at mealtime the horn that sounds for the gathering of the clans, morning noon and night, always finds a score of irrepressible, exultant wanderers miles away in remote fastnesses of the earth, exploring the azure depths of ice caverns in the bowels of Nesqually Glacier [the spelling of "Nisqually" varied at the time] or poised on a dizzy ledge of rocks studying the strange ways of the whistling marmot. Nevertheless, . . . it was ascertained that 200 people accepted the invitation of the Mazamas and were encamped in Paradise Park, Mt. Rainier, between July 16 and August 1. So notable a representation of American brain, brawn and pluck, intent upon storming a great snow-peak, was never before seen on a mountain-side. . . .

The piquant and blood-firing ceremonials of the Sierra Club were a revelation in merry-making to the Mazamas—the humorous masquerade, gay pantomimes, impromptu songs, quick volleys of repartee shot forth from a hundred throats as with one voice, turned our mountain camp-fires into opera bouffe that would have done credit to the brightest and drollest comedians in the land. Much of this came from Berkeley and Stanford college wits, for these two universities had sent a strong delegation to the mountain. . . . And the Mazamas, catching the Sierra spirit of fun, returned this fusillade with fervor. . . . The twenty-seven Appalachians, cultured, gentle-mannered New Englanders of the finest type, who had come a distance of four thousand miles, and were encamped with the Sierra Club, generously surrendered to us their leader [club president], Dr. Charles E. Fay of Tufts College, Mass. . . .

When the great day [for the summit climb] arrived and everybody's boots had been properly spiked with jagged looking screws for the ice-work, it was a fantastic but resolute crowd that assembled. . . . No word had been spoken, yet it had been tacitly understood by the more experienced men in camp that it was a hazardous feat to take so large a company of young women around Gibraltar, the majority of them college girls wholly untried in mountain work above 8,000 feet elevation. The danger from falling rocks was one that could not be guarded against; moreover, a bit of hysterical nervousness from one member of the party (not uncommon at such high altitude) might easily prove contagious to a score of others at a critical juncture. . . .

The Mazama's invitation: "Come one, come all."

Every precaution, therefore, had been taken by the outing committee for the safety of those entrusted to their care. And it may be said here, in passing, that all the young women who left Camp Muir for the summit on Wednesday, July 26th, displayed a calmness and self-poise in the face of peril, as well as rugged power of endurance, that spoke well for Western womanhood. . . . [The group climbed] under strict military discipline, all having signed a formal agreement to obey orders. On the way they met the sixty-one Sierrans just returning to camp in Paradise Valley from the conquest of the summit; and there in those vast snow-fields stretching upward to the highest peak in the United States they paused a moment to exchange greetings.

"Hi, Hi!

Sierra, Sierra,

Woh!" shouted the homeward bound conquerors, and ringing clearly across the snow came the response,

"Wah, Hoo, Wah!

Wah, Hoo, Wah!

Billy goat, nannie goat,

Ma-za-ma!"

From the late 1890s until the early 1920s, outdoor clubs hiked and climbed in large groups. Few people had their own tents, sleeping bags, or cooking kits until after World War I, when army surplus gear became available; lightweight outfits and comfortable backpacks belonged decades into the future. Snapshots here are from Mountaineers' albums. This one is "On top," 1915.

"Two yumps," 1919

A large expedition to Rainier came six years later. Two hundred members of Portland's Mazama club rode the train to Tacoma and traveled on to the Mountain by stage: solitude had given way to mass pleasure. Forty-five tents blossomed at Paradise. Packers unloaded four tons of supplies, then turned the horses out to graze along with two beef cows and seven milk cows.

Fifty-eight campers climbed to the summit, including Fay Fuller, making her second climb. Professor Edgar McClure from the University of Oregon also climbed—and died. Rainier had claimed its first climbing fatality. "An expert on elevations," the professor carried a three-foot mercury barometer strapped across his back while descending by moonlight, and it may have caught against something and thrown him off balance. He fell from a promontory, now named McClure Rock. A saddened colleague worked with McClure's readings and calculated the Mountain's height as 14,528 feet, which was close to the two immediately previous readings (though more than a hundred feet higher than today's officially accepted elevation of 14,410 feet).

Packing up, 1915: "How such delicacies as hot oyster soup, Porterhouse steak, cream potatoes, flapjacks, and peach pie could be evolved from that packtrain of ugly little cayuse ponies . . . will ever be an unsolved problem."

After McClure's tragedy, an increased awareness of danger wove a dark thread into Rainier outings—but without dimming their ebullience. The Mazamas returned to Paradise in 1905, joined by members of California's Sierra Club, the Appalachian Mountain Club, and a representative of the American Alpine Club. These four clubs comprised the complete roster of America's major outdoor clubs at the time. (Seattle's Mountaineers did not form until the next year.) Campfires lit the nights at Paradise. Clubs competed by performing skits, and seventy-five

"Planting edelweiss," 1912: No one worried about introducing a non-native species, although the edelweiss they planted in the Summerland–Glacier Basin area seems not to have survived.

marksmen indulged in a snowball fight. Hazard Stevens, a brigadier general in the Civil War, commanded one side. Now in his sixties, he had come to climb the Mountain again as celebration of the thirty-fifth anniversary of his pioneering ascent with Philemon Van Trump. Campers praised him in a song set to the tune of "John Brown's Body":

Glory be to General Stevens,
Glory be to General Stevens,
Glory be to General Stevens,
The first man on the top.

The 1905 outing held certain portents of the future: Scientists and professors in the group gave natural history talks and led discussions, forerunners of the naturalists' programs that became a national park hallmark. Stephen Mather, a millionaire Sierra Club member of the 1905 outing, would become the first director of the National Park Service. And photographer Asahel Curtis would begin a three-decade involvement as what historian Theodore Catton terms Mount Rainier's "most active and informed private citizen." Curtis served as the Park Company's first chief mountain guide. He applied unsuccessfully to become the National Park Service superintendent. And

despite that defeat, he exerted immense influence on the park for decades by heading a group of prominent Seattle and Tacoma businessmen, which formed the Rainier National Park Advisory Board.

The same year that the Rainier National Park Company stirred to life as the park's exclusive concessionaire (1916), the newly formed Cooperative Campers of the Pacific Northwest also came to Mount Rainier. The two organizations' parentage could scarcely have differed more. The Seattle-Tacoma business community fathered the Company. Anna Louise Strong founded the Cooperative Campers. With a doctorate in social work, Strong was a notable activist in the politically charged years surrounding World War I. A radical, a liberal, and a populist, she clearly was *not* the business community's ideal woman. Her outdoor club, which leaned to the left politically, welcomed anyone who seemed likely to be "a good camper" and paid one dollar to join. By-laws stated the organization's goals: "to encourage the love of simple living in the open air, and to make the wonders of our Mountains accessible." Groups of up to twenty-five people hiked from camp to camp, staying as long as they liked at sites that circled more than halfway around Rainier: Paradise, Ohanapecosh Park, Summerland, Glacier Basin, Mystic

"Coming down," 1915

Imogen Cunningham and Roi Partridge

Photographer Imogen Cunningham (1883–1976), renowned for portraits and studies of plants, initially taught herself photography through a correspondence course while living on Seattle's Queen Anne Hill. She graduated from the University of Washington in 1907 and, eight years later, married Paris-trained printmaker Roi Partridge (1888–1994). Her early photographs of him created a scandal. As Imogen later commented: "[They were] made in 1915 when I was first married. You could never chase a naked husband around Mount Rainier today."

Self-portrait, 1909

Etching of Nisqually Glacier (Roi Partridge)

"We called this 'The Faun,' but I'd never call it that now. He was absolutely sitting on a sheet of ice." (Imogen Cunningham)

Lake, and Seattle Park. A non-profit charge of $1.25 a day paid for food, space in a six-person tent, blankets, a straw mattress, and the loan of specialty equipment such as alpenstocks. For a small additional charge, pack horses would carry baggage to the next camp.

This cooperative approach fell somewhere between the large outings of the Mazamas and Mountaineers, and the tent-bungalow camps and inns of the Park Company. The National Park Service worried that the Cooperative Campers might undermine the government's newly formulated concession policy, which was being tested at Mount Rainier with an eye toward applying it nationally. Anna Louise Strong had national aspirations, too. She intended to open "the far recesses of other mountain ranges and other national parks."

Instead, she followed her socialist lodestone to Moscow, and by 1923 the Cooperative Campers frayed out. Its life had been short but seminal. Was it a club or an unauthorized concession? Park Superintendent DeWitt Reaburn railed against Strong in 1918, saying that "she is spending absolutely nothing in the way of developing, but expects the Service to do a lot of things in the way of fixing up and improving conditions. . . ." How *should* public

enjoyment be facilitated: through the investment of private capital or the expenditure of public funds?

Strong herself recognized that "due to the inevitable comparison with the standards they see about them" at Paradise, not all Cooperative Campers were happy. "[P]eople who ride up in autos expect a different type of camp-life from those who walk." To resolve the dilemma, the Cooperative Campers decided to close their Paradise camp and concentrate on operating in the park's roadless back country. That pointed to another dilemma. How should park back country be differentiated from front country?

The Park Service decided in 1922 to limit the Cooperative Campers to 100 persons, maximum, at any one site—a great shift from the immediately previous 200-plus throngs of the mountaineering clubs. At the same time, Assistant Director Arno Cammerer wrote of a need to "get the greatest number of people to visit certain sections of the parks that have been opened up." The Service provided free public campgrounds, supplying water, toilets, chopped wood, and evening programs. The era of catering to people with their own tents and cooking gear—and automobiles—had begun.

Widespread ownership of automobiles changed how people came to the park and also stimulated the development of public campgrounds, such as the one at Ohanapecosh.

Skiers and snowshoers reached Paradise on foot when the road was closed to vehicles. The park super-intendent's 1937-38 report mentions a need "to meet the demands of winter sports enthusiasts" and applauds the director's approval of plans for a new ski lodge. Broken and sprained ankles and knees that year numbered 127; the Park Company employed a full-time doctor.

The Park Company hoped skiing would provide a needed financial boost.

Big-Time Skiing

In the 1930s the public, the Park Company, and the Park Service quite clearly wanted the same thing: skiing. Skiing had begun in America with a 1905 tournament in Michigan which featured a Suicide Hill jump. Mount Rainier's involvement started in 1912, when fifty Mountaineers eager for a weekend of snow play at Longmire trudged into the park from the end of the rail line at Ashford. One member of the party carried skis, and the rest carried snowshoes. Three years later, Tacoman Thor Bisgard led fellow Mountaineers on the first cross-country ski trip to Paradise. Other club leaders still distrusted skis and insisted on snowshoes, but Bisgard's flock of loyalists quickly grew. In 1916 a ski tournament dominated the slopes of Paradise—and Scandinavians dominated the tournament. World amateur champion Nels Nelson soared 240 feet from the jump at the top of Alta Vista.

Paradise Inn opened in 1917, and that same year the Mountaineers arranged with the Park Company to rent rooms for their winter outing. Neither the road to Paradise nor the inn was open to the public, but the Mountaineers

skied and snowshoed their way up through the snow—and supplied their own food. "Our commissary had been sent in on horseback three months before, and cached in a . . . snow bank," wrote club member L.A. Nelson. "No heat was in the bedrooms, candles were used, except in the dining room, where oil lamps were a luxury. Our cooks prepared the meals but the men of the party sawed all the fireplace wood. . . . [M]usic and laughter around the fireplaces; a daily newspaper was published, good fellowship, joy in the outdoor life and appreciation of its beauty abounded."

In 1920 hearty Rainier enthusiasts calling themselves the SOYPs (Socks Outside Your Pants) also made winter Paradise pilgrimages. They herringboned up the slopes and schussed down by day, and they spent the nights in rollicking camaraderie. Members constituted the Puget Sound elite: Frederick Padelford, Thomas Stimson, Philip Weyerhaeuser, Keith Bullitt, Frank Lamb, Everett and Herbert Griggs, Carl Gould, Winlock Miller, Robert Walkinshaw, Asahel Curtis, as well as Park Superintendent Owen Tomlinson, Park Company Manager Thomas Martin, and

Paradise skier Olive Rand of Tacoma, who borrowed skis for the 1917 Mountaineers' trek, described them as "two lanky slabs of wood, with turned-up ends and a pair of simple loops for harness which quite failed to keep the runners straight, or for that matter on [the] feet at all."

future manager Paul Sceva. While on these outings, the men used only "mountain names" for one another: Tip-soo, Tatoosh, Ohanapecosh, Klickitat, TumTum, Wow, Sluiskin, Owhi. They printed the *Book of SOYP*, illustrated with Curtis's photographs, which recounts adventures and includes the group's multi-verse song. Its refrain repeats:

Hail to you, Oh SOYPs most dear!
Here we come another year,
Toiling up the long white way
From the valleys far away.

Clothing and boots for hiking and climbing served also for skiing. Even boots with soles studded by tricouni nails doubled as ski boots: one simply(?) placed a metal plate over the nails to protect the wooden surface of the skis. Equipment had to be ordered from European catalogs, until Eddie Bauer stores began importing and retailing skis in the late 1920s. By 1930 Frederick & Nelson advertised that its golf shop had added skis for the winter season, and the University Book Store offered laminated hickory skis for $7.50 a pair. In 1935 Alf Nydin of Seattle founded *Ski Magazine,* which was the first magazine devoted to the sport.

Public enthusiasm pressured the Park Service to plow the road above Longmire farther and farther, toward Paradise. By 1932 the road stayed open as far as Narada Falls. And in April 1934, the Seattle *Post-Intelligencer* sponsored a Silver Skis Race, the first of what would become an annual event. The race course reached from Camp Muir to near Paradise Inn, four and a half miles, with an elevation drop of 4,662 feet. The overall pitch figured out at 33 percent. The winner, Don Fraser, crossed the finish line in just over nine minutes.

All contestants started at the same time that first year, causing pandemonium and creating a hazard that was corrected in subsequent years. The races continued through 1941, with the exception of 1937. That year storms had "brought the worst weather conditions for any month of April during the past fifteen years," as the park superintendent reported to the National Park Service director in May. Back to Hollywood went Sonia Heine and Tyrone Power, who had been at Paradise for the filming of *Thin Ice.* The weather shut down production. It also cancelled the 1937 Silver Skis, which the superintendent had termed "the classic event of the United States." For a week, skiers had been practicing the slopes "and they, without exception, pronounced the course and conditions . . . the most perfect they had ever seen." The weather caused a twenty-four-hour postponement, then cancellation, because of "the stormy conditions which prevailed over three-fourths of the upper part of the course." Disappointment reigned, but the entrants, many of them "the best skiers from Austria, Norway, Sweden, Canada and the United States" vol-

After the 1935 Olympic trials, the Tacoma *News Tribune* gleefully predicted that Paradise would "be the skiing center of America in five years and one of the outstanding spots for the sport in the world in a decade." The article spoke of "Mount Tacoma," not Mount Rainier, even though the name controversy supposedly had been settled eighteen years earlier.

unteered to entertain "with short slalom runs, jumping, and ski stunts. In fact, the exhibition was more spectacular and entertaining to the visitors than the Silver Skis Race would have been."

The National Ski Association used the lower two-thirds of the Silver Ski course for its national championship downhill and slalom races. In December 1934, the same year as the first Silver Ski Race, the National Champion Race brought 2,000 cars into the park, carrying 7,500 spectators who hiked the final mile to Paradise to watch and cheer. Three wire services described the excitement for newspapers, the Columbia Broadcasting System carried live coverage, and newsreels filled the screens of theaters across America.

The Park Service considered winter sport to be Rainier's "most important public use," and Stephen Mather singled out the park as the nation's most suitable winter playground. It had ample snow, which lasted into summer, and a growing population that lived close by. Public interest in skiing also justified spending public money to plow the road and provide other services. Mather listened to Paul Sceva's plea that the Park Company needed an aerial tram from Narada to Paradise (one of the shortest trams suggested by recurring proposals). And he listened to the park superintendent's recital of realities, issues such as inadequate parking space, dealing with injuries, and concern for avalanche danger.

The issues applied not only to Paradise, but increasingly also to the east side of the Mountain. During the winter of 1937–38, almost 35,000 skiers drove to Cayuse Pass on weekends, and the Park Service asked the Mountaineers to please conduct their winter outing from Cayuse Pass to

Donald W. Fraser: The Ski Race of All Time

Donald W. Fraser, a Northwest pioneer skier, won the Silver Skis race in 1934 and 1938, and was on the U.S. Olympic ski team in 1936. He married Gretchen Kunigk, of Tacoma, who won gold and silver medals in the 1948 Winter Olympics, the first medals ever won by an American woman skier.

The 1934 Silver Skis race was a classic. Downhill skiing was just getting started in the U.S. and was barely off the ground in Europe. . . . A few ski and mountaineering clubs, such as the Seattle Ski Club, the Mountaineer's Washington Ski Club, and some Canadian ski clubs put on minor races for downhill, but nothing of any magnitude. Then the Seattle *P-I* newspaper, along with the backing of Seattle and Portland sports enthusiasts, decided to put on the ski race of all time. They finally decided on Camp Muir to Paradise Valley as the race course—approximately five miles long, with a vertical drop of 5,000 feet. There was great newspaper and radio publicity, which attracted competitors and some 5,000 spectators. Race day arrived and it was absolutely beautiful. A perfectly clear day with no wind, which is rare. We left Paradise shortly after daylight for the two-and-one-half- to three-hour trek to Camp Muir. . . .

We lined up, spread across the Muir Glacier, possibly ten to twenty feet apart, in all different kinds of what we called "ski gear"—from riding breeches and corduroy pants to gabardine knickers and jumping suits. Skis were a motley variety, too, both with and without metal edges. I used a pair of Northland seven-foot nine-inch triple-grooved hickory jumping skis without edges, but with lead slabs nailed on top for additional weight. . . .

Otto Sanford fired his starting pistol, and approximately sixty-four of us started off simultaneously down the Muir Glacier. Some of us shot straight down the fall line toward Paradise. Others chose to zigzag their way down. The snow was hard and the surface mostly ice. About half the time, one was airborne due to the depressions and ridges, and my heavy, stiff jumping skis with the added lead weights were not the best choice.

Fortunately, I was soon out in front of the mob, so I didn't witness the many terrible collisions that took place just behind me. One in particular—between Ben Thompson, a Mount Rainier summit guide and partner in Anderson and Thompson skis, and Stan Borgerson—resulted in a badly broken jaw for Ben and a dislocated shoulder for Stan. Hans Otto Giese had a smashing collision with another racer (name forgotten), and each berated the other, claiming right-of-way, while precious seconds went ticking by.

Between McClure Rock and Panorama Point there were large mounds (like jumping hills), and skiers were airborne 100 feet or more on each one. The speed at this point was far more than any of us had ever known before—even on a jumping hill. Tired legs took their toll. I had my only fall at this point and minutes went by trying to unravel. It was then that Carlton Wiegel caught up with me. From there on . . . , through snow that was by now mostly mush, we skied side by side, and it was only when we approached the finish line that my cross-country training made the difference and I was able to finish a few feet ahead of Carlton.

What a race! From 10,000 feet at Camp Muir to 5,000 at Paradise, with the winning time just over nine minutes. Sixty-four competitors with a simultaneous start. From ice at the top to slush at the bottom.

(Left) The caption for this snapshot reads: "Do you think you have troubles? Try this for jangled nerves and mental stress." From 1934 to 1975, a concessionaire operated rope tows at Paradise. Now, the area is open for cross-country skiing, snowshoeing, and snow play, a return to original non-mechanized types of winter use.

(Right) "Thousands of skiers swarmed over the slopes of Mount Rainier last week-end, as the Rainier National Park Company made winter facilities available for the first time since before the war." Seattle *Times*, December 2, 1946

(Below) Skis devised in 1937 by Trail Foreman Bob Jeffrey for use while on winter elk patrol at Three Lakes

Tipsoo Lake without fanfare. If skiers en masse discovered Tipsoo, how could the National Park Service keep pace with the need to provide shelter, sanitation, and safety? There was Sunrise, too. Clubs on the northwest side of the Mountain, from Seattle to Enumclaw, wanted winter access to the facilities at Sunrise—and maybe a tram.

"Skiing is like the measles!" wrote Ralph A. Spencer, a Tacoma high-school student, in *Scholastic,* the newsletter widely used by schools to encourage reading. "I was exposed about three years ago . . . [and] the craze spread among my friends, just as it is still spreading over the country."

But warnings were sounded. The national park's landscape architect, Ernest A. Davidson, summarized a concern: "There is a point where a fine, healthy outdoor sport begins to degenerate. This point is reached when the majority of its so-called devotees are more interested in the various side-lines of the sport than they are in the sport itself; when the sport becomes the social thing-to-do, rather than the

athletic thing to be done. . . . At Mt. Rainier this point is dangerously near."

The question of suitability, plus the disruption of World War II, punctured the momentum for developing Paradise as a premier ski resort. The Park Service decided against major, permanent lifts inside the park, and the Park Company did not want to finance a demountable T-bar lift. Policy in some years kept the road to Paradise open and the rope tows running; in other years, it vetoed them. Ski developments at White Pass, Crystal, the Snoqualmie area, Stevens Pass, and Mount Baker gained favor.

Mount Rainier's deep, white blanket and immense winter beauty are again a domain for cross-country skiing and playful sliding and snowball-throwing. And although hi-tech clothing and gear separate today's winter visitors from those of yesterday, in spirit many of those who now trek to Paradise are more akin to the excursionists of the early outings than to the racers and jumpers of the park's skiing glory days.

Northwesterners snowshoed at Rainier before skis gained popularity. "On we mushed again, going up the road, breaking trail to Paradise Valley," wrote University of Washington Professor Milnor Roberts in a 1909 *National Geographic* article.

The 1920s and early '30s winter pilgrimages of the SOYPs included games of snowshoe baseball. At the end of their annual sojourns, reported the *Book of SOYP,* "amid many sighs of regret but nevertheless filled with health and inspiration . . . the tribe [would] mush back to the haunts of war."

Descending above the clouds with only Little Tahoma in view, 1950s

Alma Wagen, of whom fellow-guide Erroll Rawson commented: "Here's our lady guide. She never took any summit trips by herself. She wasn't very fond of the summit trip. She liked . . . Pinnacle Peak and around [there]."

To the Top!

"Only women accustomed to rugged exercise and endowed with robust health, clear heads, and good lungs should attempt to reach the summit," cautioned the leaflet announcing the Mazama's 1897 outing to Mount Rainier. They should "avoid wearing too much clothing, as it soon occasions fatigue," but should be sure to have "very strong shoes," warm underwear, and wool bloomers, not skirts. "Much of the route is across loose boulders, where skirts, even though short, would endanger the wearer's life."

In 1905, after a successful outing, the Mazama's journal marveled at how well the women in the party had done. Put to the test, they actually "displayed a calmness and self-poise . . . that spoke well for Western womanhood. Although one of them fainted, . . . she quickly recovered herself and continued resolutely to the top."

Three generations later, the 1990s job description for climbing rangers does not mention gender. What counts is: "excellent physical condition to climb throughout the wilderness of the park and to perform lengthy search and rescue missions, emergency medical service, [and] wilderness patrols. . . ." The "incumbent" can expect to work in "very hazardous mountainous terrain typified by glaciers, snowfields, and steep rock and ice slopes . . . [which are] subject to cold, windy, snowy conditions for 6 to 8 months each year." Rainier has become a his/her mountain.

The hazards of climbing can be great. Fate depends not just on mountaineering experience and determination, but also on weather and ice conditions. In his autobiography, 1990s chief guide Lou Whittaker, tells: "I was kicking steps and all of a sudden I felt weightless. . . . I felt the rope tighten around my waist and suddenly realized that I'd fallen into a crevasse." Whittaker and his rope of three other climbers, along with a second rope of three, had reached the 13,000-foot level on the Cowlitz Glacier. They were fighting a stiff wind that blew snow in their faces and restricted visibility. Snow hiding a crevasse gave way beneath Whittaker's weight and he fell with the snow and a chunk of ice, which gave him "the sensation of being on a descending elevator." When the rope arrested his fall, Whittaker realized he was dangling about twenty feet down, held by his waist belt. Even by penduluming his body, he could not reach either wall to climb out because the lips of this particular crevasse were too overhung. He

Prominent Seattle architect Carl F. Gould, a member of the Mountaineers, designed the Camp Muir hut, which was built in 1916. With Asahel Curtis sparking the request, the club six years earlier had urged construction of two high-camp shelters: one below Gibraltar Rock (Camp Muir) and another at Steamboat Prow. Lack of a shelter contributed to Edgar McClure's death in 1897. Because of a storm, he elected to descend at night rather than bivouac.

Climbing above Little Tahoma, Emmons Route

was suspended in mid-space, his rope held by the other climbers. They had driven their ice axes into the snow, using the self-arrest position he had taught them just the day before.

Someone had borrowed Whittaker's ascenders, the devices intended to solve this kind of situation. These are strong cord footloops, fitted with metal grippers that can be slid by hand up a rope while shifting weight from one foot to the other. Lacking ascenders, Whittaker considered dropping off the rope and "trying to crawl along the bottom of the crevasse to the end," hoping for a wedge of ice to climb up. But 100 feet of emptiness gaped between his feet and the crevasse bottom.

After ten minutes had passed, the second rope of climbers reached the scene and called down, asking what to do. Whittaker told them to untie, drop one end of their rope down to him—and secure the other end! By making

a loop on the end of the new rope and passing it under his climbing belt, Whittaker could put one foot in the loop. From it, he could transfer weight to a substitute ascender fashioned by tying the drawstring cord of his pack to the rope he dangled from. With a prusik knot, the loop would not slip when weighted, but could easily be slid up when unweighted. Using the two loops, Whittaker climbed up one step at a time. Standing in the loop of the second rope, he slid the knot, and the climbers at the surface pulled in slack on the first rope. Then he transferred his weight back to the prusik loop, and they pulled in slack on the second rope. Outcome? Re-emergence at the glacier's surface. No harm done.

Other, equally experienced climbers have died on Mount Rainier. Willi Unsoeld, a renowned and beloved climber, successfully reached the summit of Mount Everest in 1963 but was killed by an avalanche on Rainier in

1964. A professor at The Evergreen State College in Olympia, Unsoeld was leading an Outdoor Education class on a leisurely snow excursion to the high slopes in late February. Severe weather halted the group after they had climbed to about 13,000 feet, and they returned to their tents a thousand feet lower. Snow fell through the night and buried the camp beneath three or four feet of white fluff. The climbers started down in the morning, their feet sinking deep with each step, more snow falling, and the wind blasting at sixty miles an hour. Unsoeld led the first rope, with Janie Diepenbrock behind him, then Peter Miller, then Frank Kaplan. Five other ropes followed, spaced 100 feet apart.

Miller thought he saw Diepenbrock fall and immediately dropped into an arrest position. Actually, she had not fallen. She had been pulled over the fracture line of a slab avalanche, which struck Unsoeld. The whole slope slid, pulling Miller and Kaplan, too. When the avalanching snow stopped, all four lay buried. Kaplan had managed to shed his pack and "swim" while the snow was moving. This kept him near the surface. He freed himself and peered through the storm for signs of other survivors. He spot-

Fixing dinner amid the stone windbreaks at Camp Curtis, near Steamboat Prow

As dawn begins to tint the sky and the snow-covered ice, mountain guide Dick McGowan leads a 1950s party that has already been underway for about three hours.

ted Miller's hand protruding above the avalanche's surface and went to him. Miller had opened an air space around his nose and mouth before the snow had stopped moving and set into a rigid solid. He had also thrust up an arm as high as he could. That saved his life: along with "swimming," the breathing space, and the upthrusting of an arm are rules one through three of what to do if caught by an avalanche.

Kaplan started digging with his hands and freed Miller's face. The other teams caught up. Some helped dig, using light shovels carried as snow-camp equipment. Others followed the rope downslope, looking for Diepenbrock and Unsoeld—a slow task because the rope lay partly buried at considerable depth, and its course was not straight. They found Janie Diepenbrock two feet below the surface, apparently dead. Nonetheless—to no avail—they began artificial resuscitation while continuing to dig.

Farther downslope and beneath three feet of snow, they found Willi Unsoeld. Forty-five minutes had passed since the avalanche struck. All the students could do was remove the pack from his back, take out the Park Service radio he carried, and report the tragedy to rangers at Paradise. The nineteen survivors then staggered on to Camp Muir. Everybody had done everything exactly right. Fate had intervened.

Waiting for help, the students composed a song to give words to their shock and to celebrate their deeply loved professor of philosophy and religion: "You can't kill a spirit. It goes on and on."

"Paradise to Summit 4 hours 50 min," wrote guides Dick McGowan and Gil Blinn in the climbers' register kept in a metal box at the summit. That was on July 30, 1959. They had started from Paradise at midnight and were back there, ready for breakfast, at 6:40 the next morning. On top again two days later with clients, McGowan and Blinn added the elapsed time of their July 30 return to Paradise: "1 hr 50 min." For years, that roundtrip time of 6 hours and 40 min-

Ted Kerstetter: "RUN TO YOUR RIGHT!"

Ted Kerstetter, a retired zoology professor, survived the 1981 tragedy on the upper Ingraham Glacier—the worst disaster in American alpine history in terms of the number of lives lost.

The weather was unsettled as we hiked from Paradise to Camp Muir the day before our try for the summit. But patches of blue showed between the racing clouds and we felt at least semi-optimistic that the climb would go. What better way to celebrate Father's Day 1981 than to stand on top of the Northwest's premier mountain!

Dinner that night at Camp Muir was basic carbo-loading fare—mounds of spaghetti heaped on our plates, washed down with plenty of liquid. We were in our sleeping bags early, but sleep was slow in coming. The guide's hut was congested, jam-packed, a symphony of snores until the wake-up call at 1:00 a.m. Departure was set for 2:00. My wife Gayle, our 19-year-old son Greg, and I sleepily pulled on layers of polyester, wool, and goosedown, strapped on crampons and headlamps, and tied into climbing ropes in teams of four or five (the three of us on three different ropes). Our group, twenty-nine altogether, headed out in single file—six rope teams slowly crossing the Cowlitz Glacier toward Cadaver Gap and the Ingraham Glacier beyond. After a couple hours, three climbers decided this was not for them; they returned to Camp Muir with one of the guides.

By dawn we were at 12,300 feet on the Ingraham Glacier, a long tongue of ice dropping from far up the mountain to an icefall, a tangled mass of broken ice and snow flowing over a high cliff. Partway across the glacier the chief guide halted the long string of us and, with two fellow guides, continued upslope to reconnoiter the route ahead. The rest of us sat on the snow, facing downslope and inspecting an enormous crevasse a hundred yards below us, watching the beauty of the sunrise, and enjoying the respite.

Only a muted thunder building in intensity behind us broke our reverie. We turned almost in unison to see a wall of snow and ice plummeting down the glacier directly toward us. The icefall had given away. The sight remains burned into my memory. In that moment I knew I was dead, that my life had come to its end. But the instinct to survive takes over and a shout from far across the glacier—"Run to your right! Run to your right!"—galvanized me. I was on my feet in an instant, running clumsily, crampons and heavy clothing slowing my frantic efforts to escape the oncoming avalanche. Within seconds the first of the debris struck, tossing and rolling me downslope, pounding me with chunks of ice and snow as I went. My only thought was: "Please, make it fast. Please, not a slow suffocating death." As if in answer to my plea, a huge piece of flying ice struck between my shoulder blades, momentarily stunning me with pain. Then—quiet.

I lay face down, amazed to be alive and desperately trying to catch my breath for, what, a moment? a minute? ten minutes? Truthfully, I have no idea. But eventually, painfully, I struggled to my feet and climbed slowly

Professor Jonathan Laitone photographed the dawn, moments before the 1981 avalanche struck and killed him. Of the disaster victims, his father wrote: "It covered them with 3,000 feet of ice. They remain there today, in their fantastic mausoleum." He also wrote: "His camera was knocked out of his hands. Rangers found it days later and made prints of all of Jonathan's photos. His Calif. driver's license no. was etched onto the camera, but he was listed as an Ann Arbor, Mich., resident. It took many more days before I received his damaged (I could not repair it) camera, and photos."

upslope toward three or four other climbers looking dazed as they surveyed the aftermath. Greg was among them.

"We lost ten," he said.

"How do you know?" I asked.

"I counted. There were twenty-one of us resting on the glacier. Now there are only eleven." (He was almost right; actually there were twenty-two on the glacier; eleven died.)

We spotted Gayle. She had been pushed perilously close to the yawning crevasse we sat observing only minutes ago. Now it was filled with avalanche debris and the bodies of eleven of our comrades. The guides searched frantically, shouting and listening. Only silence. Clouds descended and thickened, darkening the scene.

The trip back down the mountain was slow, somber, painful, much of it in the zero visibility of a whiteout. Separated ribs made deep breathing impossible for me; others bled through bandages covering head wounds, and limping gaits testified to leg injuries. Emotional wounds were

worse. Friends lost friends. Two Seattle brothers went up together; one returned. The pregnant wife of a young Pennsylvania man gave him the trip as a Father's Day gift; he didn't return to her. A twenty-seven-year-old, full-professor mechanical engineer from Michigan died. He had written satirical comedy, designed a solar heating system for his church, and planned to study for a master's degree in art. An apprentice guide, twenty-one years old, newly graduated from college and looking forward to a year of study in Europe, was lost. We thought of these matters as we descended. I also thought of the guide who yelled "Run to your right!" Had that saved lives? Almost certainly. Regrettably, I never identified and thanked him.

Two days later Gayle and I dropped Greg off at SeaTac airport, his expedition backpack carrying everything he would need for six months of work and travel in Alaska. Life went on—for some of us.

Resting high on the Ingraham Glacier

Sunburn plagues climbers because of thin atmosphere and high reflectance from the glacier surface. Zinc oxide, if applied adequately and in time, prevents most burns.

utes held the speed record. But in 1981, and again in 1982, climbing guide Craig Van Hoy made a roundtrip from Paradise in 5 hours and 20 minutes. In 1985, Ken Evans and Matt Christensen shaved another eleven minutes off the record. The usual climb entails hiking from Paradise to Camp Muir at the 10,000-foot level one day, getting up about 2:00 a.m. the next morning, and climbing for six to eight hours to reach the summit, then using up another three to four descending back to Muir. Twenty-nine formally recognized routes have been successfully climbed since 1855.

By somewhere around 11,000 feet, the exertion forces many climbers' to begin gasping or hyperventilating. The lack of oxygen, due to increasing altitude, nauseates others. Lifting a hand to scratch the forehead may not seem worth the effort. Each added step becomes an act of will. Even the cheerful words "almost there" ring hollow. But how else amid the green latitudes of our city lives can one experience the white and blue and black world of nothing but ice and sky and rock? Through 1998, the number of climbers to reach the summit has totaled more than 120,000. About 5,000 people per year now stand on top.

Entries from the summit register, picked at random, record climbers' reactions:

- I keep thinking about a warm living room and a soft bed. Rev. Gerhard Pera, age 29.
- Nothing quite like it in the U.K. A visitor from England, Mike Rees.
- Greetings to Captain George Vancouver and Rear Admiral Peter Rainier! Herbert Raynes, Esquimalt, B.C.
- It's windy as hell. Donald J. Fries, Tacoma.
- Get me off this damn mountain. Bruce C. Wright, Priest River, Ida.
- Look at her everyday—tried to climb twice before. Finally made it! Jack R. Morrison.
- Berg Heil! Got lost in the crater—so foggy you can't even see your nose!! 7 from B.C.
- We hit the jackpot in weather. Nonetheless, you won't see me here again. Betty D. Morse.
- Tired. Cold. Adaline, age 17.
- God! Sandahl, H. E., age 24 from Tacoma.
- If it were easy, everybody would do it! Mabel Swift, Maine.

America's Mount Everest climbers have trained at Mount Rainier, beginning with Jim Whittaker's 1962 preparation for reaching the top of the world. The two mountain mon-

A rusty baking powder tin found at the summit held records of climbs. Philomen B. Van Trump's name appears in 1879 and 1896. A business card is dated 1901. Van Trump had first climbed to the top in 1870.

(Above) Resting on the summit crater rim: a brief time to relax before starting down.

(Right) Glissading: the quick and easy way to descend, where possible, if legs and knees are not too fatigued.

(Opposite page) How to welcome today's climbers, hikers, skiers, and sightseers, yet also safeguard the park for future visitors is a dilemma facing officials and public alike. What will Mount Rainier's second hundred years as a park bring?

archs share snow, ice, and wind, as well as weather that swings capriciously from fog or blizzard to blazing sun. Climbers do not need oxygen masks on Rainier, but they can test them on its slopes for fit and ease of use. Zippers that freeze and lock into immobility can be identified and redesigned, parka lengths can be adjusted, expedition foods can be sampled and accepted or given a thumbs-down.

This Rainier-for-the-climbing-elite is fully matched or even excelled in spirit by Rainier-for-the-aged-the-young-and-the-infirm. In 1929 a ninety-one-year-old man attempted a climb, failed, and asked for his money back. The Park Company refused; he had been warned. In 1978 Julius Boehm, the well-known Issaquah candymaker, climbed to the top at age eighty; he even sang a few bars from *Der Rosenkavalier* enroute. In 1992, at age eighty-one, Jack Borgenicht of New Jersey bested Boehm's age record. At the other end of the age scale, future Washington governor Dixy Lee Ray climbed the Mountain at age twelve, and in 1972, seven-year-old Laurie Johnson of Tacoma also reached the top. She climbed with her parents and three siblings (ages eleven, thirteen, and fifteen).

In 1922 amputee Ellery Walter, who wrote a travel book entitled *The World on One Leg,* aspired to climb Rainier but was turned down. He wanted four rangers to help him "on dangerous sections of the trail . . . and over the snow bridges and around crevasses, and to carry necessary food and camp supplies for spending two nights in the open." In 1978 one-legged Jack Graves climbed the Mountain and skied alone from the summit down the Ingraham Glacier. The Park Service fined him fifty dollars. He had neither a permit for a solo climb nor the required experience. What he did have were determination and a Seattle prosthetics business. He had designed his own artificial leg specifically for climbing and skiing.

In 1981 Jim Whittaker (helped by fourteen others) led a party of handicapped climbers. Eleven made it to the top; two turned back just below 12,000 feet. Handicaps in the group ranged from blindness and deafness to epilepsy and the loss of a leg. The blind climbers were less bothered by precarious heights than were the sighted climbers. During a rope suspension traverse, one blind climber asked how far above the surface she was, and when told "about 120 feet," she quipped, "Okay. I won't look down."

Why climb? Maybe John Muir had the answer when he wrote: "I didn't mean to climb it, but got excited and soon was on top." The simple truth is that Mount Rainier's magnificent bulk draws human bodies, minds, and souls. Its story reaches far back in time—and far into the future.

Tomorrow

For the Mountain, one century means little. It is too fleeting a moment. Not so for people. Excursionists at the time of the park's birth set subalpine groves on fire simply for the nighttime spectacle of flames and sparks, and a committee of devoted Mountaineers sent to Switzerland for edelweiss seeds to add still more glory to Rainier's already lovely gardens.

In the 1890s, two to three hundred people every year visited the park. By the 1990s, the figure stood at two million—a ten-thousand-fold increase. Cars once revolutionized park patterns by bringing people to the park on their own schedules. Now they bring too many. Arrive on a sunny Sunday in summer and the odds of stopping at Paradise are far from assured. All parking lots are likely to be full. Furthermore, even without circling there fruitlessly, cars affect the park. Their exhaust fumes gray the skies and influence the Mountain's ecosystems.

Park superintendent Bill Briggle muses about the flow of one century into the next. "We can't re-do yesterday," he says, "and today is gone. What we can do is get a handle on tomorrow. We need to communicate about volcanic hazards. We don't know when, and we don't know what or where. But we do know this mountain will erupt, disgorge mud, or flood torrentially again. Always has. Always will."

Yet today's public shows scant willingness to recognize their Mountain as a threat and adjust their approach to it. This, despite Mt. Saint Helens' recent demonstration of destructive power and despite Park Service transportation and campground alternatives suggested in the current twenty-year management plan. "The public wants Rainier as they now know it—easy to access, an antidote for daily routine and stress. We need to protect those qualities but to convey also the other face of this beauty: the Mountain is a volcano.

"We have to reach into the cities and communicate the need for stewardship, too. Our visitors are better informed about national parks than ever, and our volunteers accomplish work that couldn't get done any other way. But whole segments of society do not come to the park. Their numbers will grow, and their needs and opinions and votes will determine the future. We need to communicate with that whole rainbow of today's culture."

The Mountain; the park; the people: What do they augur for the 2000s?

Suggested Reading

Barcott, Bruce. *The Measure of a Mountain: Beauty and Terror on Mount Rainier.* Seattle: Sasquatch Books, 1997. Lighthearted personal account of trips to Mount Rainier; interviews with its aficionados and researchers

Carr, Ethan. *Wilderness by Design: Landscape Architecture and the National Park Service.* Lincoln: University of Nebraska Press, 1998. Intriguing study of the history and development of American park ideals; large section devoted to Mount Rainier

Catton, Theodore. *Wonderland: An Administrative History of Mount Rainier National Park.* Seattle: National Park Service, Cultural Resources Program, 1996. An exhaustive treatise, engagingly presented

Decker, Robert W., and Barbara M. Decker. *Mountains of Fire.* Cambridge: Cambridge University Press, 1991. Excellent overview of volcanism and volcanoes

Decker, Robert W., and Barbara M. Decker. *Road Guide to Mount Rainier National Park.* Mariposa, CA: Double Decker Press, 1996. Forty-eight pages of background information plus specifics of where-to-go and what-to-see; photographs, drawings, maps

Driedger, Carolyn. *A Visitor's Guide to Mount Rainier Glaciers.* Seattle: Pacific Northwest National Parks and Forests (now Northwest Interpretive Association), 1986. Brief introduction to the Mountain's glaciers, written by an expert for the general public; photographs and line drawings

Filley, Bette. *The Fact Book about Mount Rainier.* Issaquah, WA: Dunamis House, 1996. Ambitious and extensive compilation of facts, dates, trivia, and memorabilia

Haines, Aubrey. *Mountain Fever: Historic Conquests of Mount Rainier.* Portland: Oregon Historical Society, 1962; reprinted Seattle: University of Washington Press, 1999. Comprehensive summary of the Mountain's history up to the time of the park's establishment. Well written; meticulously documented

Harris, Stephen L. *Fire and Ice: The Cascades Volcanoes.* Seattle: The Mountaineers, 1976. Somewhat dated but still valuable description of the geology and history of Northwest volcanoes; well illustrated

Kjeldsen, Jim. *The Mountaineers: A History.* Seattle: The Mountaineers, 1998. Story of a major outing club and its role in Mount Rainier National Park's development and conservation

Lyons, C. P. *Wildflowers of Washington.* Renton, WA: Lone Pine Publishing, 1997. Excellent field guide to Northwest plant identification; first published 1952, now completely revised, with information on historical botanists; color photos plus the original line drawings

Majors, Harry M., and Richard C. McCollum, editors. "Mount Rainier: The Tephra Eruption of 1894." *Northwest Discovery,* vol. 2, nos. 6 and 7, 1981. Annotated reprint of Edward S. Ingraham's winter 1894 Rainier climb, sponsored by the Seattle *Post-Intelligencer*

Martinson, Arthur D. *Wilderness Above the Sound: The Story of Mount Rainier National Park.* Flagstaff, AZ: Northland Press, 1986; reprinted, Niwot, CO: Robert Rhinehart, 1994. History of the establishment of the park

McNulty, Tim, and Pat O'Hara. *Washington's Mount Rainier National Park: A Centennial Celebration.* Seattle: The Mountaineers, 1999. Beautiful, informative portrait of the park and the Mountain, its history, geology, and ecology

Moir, William H. *Forests of Mount Rainier.* Seattle: Pacific Northwest National Parks and Forests Association (now Northwest Interpretative Association), 1989. Enjoyably written, highly informative account of the park's forests, including depictions of recovery following fire, glaciation, and mudflow

Molenaar, Dee. *The Challenge of Mount Rainier.* Seattle: The Mountaineers, 1971. Timeless tales of the ongoing urge to climb Mount Rainier; the recognized authority on this topic; many original drawings plus some photographs

Muir, John. *John Muir: The Eight Wilderness-Discovery Books.* Seattle: The Mountaineers, 1992. Collection of Muir's writings, including "An Ascent of Mount Rainier"

Nadeau, Gene Allen. *Highways to Paradise: A Pictorial History of the Roadway to Mount Rainier.* Puyallup, WA: Valley Press, 1983. Overview of the construction and historical impact of the road to Paradise, written by an Eatonville resident

Pojar, Jim, and Andy MacKinnon, compilers and editors. *Plants of Coastal British Columbia, including Washington, Oregon & Alaska.* Renton, WA: Lone Pine Publishing,

1994. Plant identification made easy; color photographs, line drawings; a definitive work

Pringle, P. T., and W. J. Gerstel, editors. *Roadside Geology of Scenic Highways at Mount Rainier National Park and Vicinity.* Olympia: Geology and Earth Resources Information Circular, Department of Natural Resources, 1999. The geological story of the Mountain written by geologists for laymen; numerous illustrations

Rohde, Jerry, and Gisela Rohde. *Mount Rainier National Park: Tales, Trails, and Auto Tours.* McKinleyville, CA: Mountain Home Books, 1996. Excellent combination guide and historical highlights, illustrated with line drawings (including renditions of historic photographs)

Schmoe, Floyd. *A Year in Paradise.* New York: Harper and Brothers, 1959; reprinted Seattle: The Mountaineers, 1999. A delightful classic; a heartfelt personal account of living at Paradise in the 1920s

Schullery, Paul. *Island in the Sky: Pioneering Accounts of Mt. Rainier, 1833–1894.* Seattle: The Mountaineers, 1987. Illustrated tales of early climbs

Sellars, Richard. *Preserving Nature in the National Parks: A History.* New Haven: Yale University Press, 1997. Perceptive discussion of changing policies within the National Park Service, from its inception to the present

Shankland, Robert. *Stephen Mather of the National Parks.* New York: McGraw Hill, 1931. Profile of first director of the National Park Service, who set the course for America's parks. He had climbed the Mountain a decade before the Park Service was established

Smoot, Jeff. *An Adventure Guide to Mount Rainier: Hiking, Climbing, and Skiing in Mount Rainier National Park.* Evergreen, CO: Chockstone Press, 1991. Short descriptions of trail hikes and off-trail routes; maps

Spring, Ira, and Harvey Manning. *50 Hikes in Mount Rainier National Park.* Seattle: The Mountaineers, 1999. Fourth edition of classic guide with updated text; all new color photographs by Ira Spring and his wife Pat, and by daughter Vicky Spring and her husband Tom Kirkendall

Steelquist, Robert, and Pat O'Hara. *A Traveler's Companion to Mount Rainier National Park.* Seattle: Pacific Northwest National Parks and Forests Association (now Northwest Interpretive Association), 1987. A forty-eight-page road guide, lavishly illustrated

Walker, Harriet K. *Around Mount Rainier with the Mountaineers, 1930: A Letter from Harriet K. Walker to Her Family.* Seattle: The Mountaineers, 1998. Warmly anecdotal, well-illustrated account of the Mountaineers' twenty-fourth summer outing at Rainier

Whittaker, Lou, and Andrea Gabbard. *Memoirs of a Mountain Guide.* Seattle: The Mountaineers, 1994. Recollections by the legendary guide and renowned climber

Credits

Cartography

Anne C. Heinitz, Washington Division of Geology and Earth Resources: xii

Illustrations

Thomas Burke Memorial Washington State Museum: 116 top right (Roi Partridge)

Imogen Cunningham Trust: 116 middle, bottom

Jerry Franklin: 45

Aubrey Haines: 49 middle left; 52 both; 53 left

Ruth and Louis Kirk: iv-v; viii; 6 top right; 7 top left; 13 right; 22 top; 23 bottom; 25 all; 31 top three, 32 top right, bottom left, and right; 33 middle left; 42-43 all; 44 top right, middle right, bottom left and right; 50; 57 top; 63 both; 64; 68 middle left; 77 top; 92 top left and right; 95 lower; 97 right; 103 middle left; 110 bottom; 117; 124; 125 right; 126; 127 both; 130 all; 132 both

Jonathan Laitone: 129

Mark Lembersky: ii; 20; 24; 27 top; 28; 29 top, 33 top right; 37 bottom; 40 top; 44 top middle; 59; 70; 71 top right; 73; 93 bottom; 94; 95 left; 99 bottom; 101 top

William Lokey: 10 top right

C. P. Lyons: 36

Robert McIntyre, Jr. (artifacts photographed by Rod Slemmons): 113 top, middle right

Bill Merrilees: 49 bottom right

Dee Molenaar: 8; 11; 12; 15; 18; 34; 89

Museum of History and Industry: 23; 123 bottom

National Park Service, Mount Rainier National Park: Artifacts photographed by Rod Slemmons: 5; 40 bottom; 75 all; 76 bottom; 77 bottom; 96 top left and right; 99 top; 101 bottom; 104 all; 107; 111; 120; 121 both; 122 bottom; 123 middle left. Photographs: 17 top and bottom left; 19; 27 bottom; 35 middle right and bottom; 66 all; 67; 68 top right and bottom; 76 middle; 80 all; 83 top; 84 bottom; 86 all; 96 bottom; 97 left; 100 both; 110 top; 112; 113; 125 left

Yoshi Nishihara: 36 middle

Dennis Olson: cover, vi, vii, x-xi, 2, 29 bottom, 32 top left, 33 bottom left, 37 top three; 38; 41 bottom; 46; 90; 108 top; 133

Patrick Pringle: 14

Royal Ontario Museum: 49 middle right (Paul Kane)

Floyd Schmoe: 26 bottom left; 44 middle left

Seattle *Times*: 17 right; 83 top; 118; 122 middle

Gordon Siebold: 33 bottom right; 44 top left

Bob and Ira Spring: 22 bottom; 85

Trygve Steen: 62

Michael Sullivan: 65 all

Temple Beth El: 4

U.S.D.A. Forest Service: 101 middle

U.S. Geological Survey: 9, 10 left

University of Washington Libraries, Collection and Preservation Division: 13 left; 21 top; 30; 35 top left; 39; 48 all; 51; 60-61 both; 67 top left and right, bottom left; 69 top right; 74; 82 top left, bottom left; 98; 114 all; 115; 122 top

Chester Vanderpool: 93

Elsie Van Eaton: 78-79

Washington Department of Natural Resources: xii

Washington State Historical Society, Special Collections Division: i; 1; 5 all except top right; 6-7 top right and middle; 10 bottom right; 21 middle left, bottom right; 23 top left; 26 top; 41 top; 49 top left and right; 50; 53 middle right, bottom right; 54; 55; 56 both; 57 bottom; 69 top left; 71 top left; 72; 75 top; 78 bottom; 79 middle; 81; 82 bottom right; 87; 88 both; 92 bottom; 119 both; 120; 131; 134

Walter and Jean Walkinshaw: 58 (George Tsutakawa)

George Yantis: 6 left

Index

Heath, Frederick, 81
Heather, xi, 36
Heine, Sonia, 6
Hemlock, western, 42
Hibernation, 27, 29
Hotels, 78, 81, 87, 101. *See also* Longmire, inns; Paradise Inn; Sunrise; Tacoma Hotel
Huckleberries, 52, 93
Hydrothermal alteration, 13

Ice Age: glaciers, 23; and treeline, 40
Ice Caves, 24, 85
Indian Henry's Hunting Ground, 76, 79, 98
Indians. *See* Native Americans
Ingraham, Edward Sturgis, 7, 12, 57, 64
Ingraham Glacier: avalanche on, 128–29
Insects, 30–31
Iyall, Bill, 50, 51, 97

Johnson, Albert, 6
Jokulhlaups. *See* Floods, outburst

Kautz, August Valentine, 50
Kautz Creek Flood, 16–17
Kautz Glacier, 32
Kent Valley mudflow, 14
Kernahan Ranch, 72
Kerstetter, Ted, 128

Lahalet, 50
Lahar. *See* Mudflows
Landscape architecture: influence of, 76, 78, 79, 87, 123
Lang, Otto, 6
LeConte, Joseph, 24, 58
Leschi, 50, 51
Levertov, Denise, 39
Little Tahoma rockfall, 13. *See also* Native Americans, myths
Lokey, Bill, 10–11
Longmire, Ben, 98
Longmire, James, 50, 51–52, 53, 64, 72
Longmire, Len, 65, 98
Longmire, Susan, 98
Longmire, Virinda, 51, 100–1
Longmire: and mudflow, 19; and mining, 65, 98, 100; inns, 71, 76, 98, 99, 100; springs, 98, 99
Lookouts. *See* Fire lookouts

McClure, Edgar, 114
McGowan, Dick, 128
McWhorter, Lucullus V., 51
Madden, John, 108
Manning, Harvey, 62, 112
Maple, vine, 42
Marine plane, 111
Marmots, 27, 29, 33, 95
Master planning, 87
Mather, Stephen T., 79, 107, 115, 120
Mazamas, 20, 13, 114, 125
Meadows, subalpine, 32–36, 40, 64–65; Native American use of, 93, 95, 97
Merriam, Dr. C. Hart, 55, 58
Metcalfe, Gertrude, 113
Milroy, Tom, 14, 16
Milwaukee Road. *See* Chicago, Milwaukee, and St. Paul Railroad
Mining, 65, 98, 100, 102
Moir, William, 42
Molenaar, Dee, 89, 111
Mount Fuji, 8, 10
Mount Rainier: as icon, vii, ix, 4; altitude of, ix, 6–8; as volcano, 8, 11–13; as hazard, 9; summit of, 10, 12, 14, 51; as training ground, 31; name of, 48, 54, 55, 56; climbers on summit, 52, 128, 131; impressions of, 131. *See also* Floods, outburst; Mount Rainier National Park; Mudflows; Wildlife policies
Mount Rainier National Park: establishment of, 20, 57–61; policies of, 74. *See also* Fire; Fire lookouts; Mount Rainier; Rainier National Park Company; Rangers; Roads; Trails
Mount Rainier Park Advisory Board, 84–85
Mount St. Helens, 9, 12, 19
"Mount Tacoma," 6, 54, 55, 56
Mountain climbing, 125–33
Mountaineering equipment, 51
Mountaineers, The, 67, 72, 87, 114, 119
Mountain goats, 32, 50, 95
Motorcycle hillclimb, 83–84
Movie-making, 6, 74
Muck-a-Muck, 52
Mudflows, 14, 19; Osceola, 13; Electron, 15–16

Muir, John: quoted, 34, 101, 133; summit climb, 47, 53
Mystic Lake, 51, 98
Myths. *See* Native Americans, myths

Naches Pass, 50
National Historic District, x, 81
National Parks: purpose of, 58, 64–68; predating Mount Rainier, 57, 64
National Ski Association, 120
Native Americans: respect for the Mountain, 6; mudflow, 14–16; myths, 14, 16, 24; fire, 41; travel routes, 50; name for the Mountain, 54, 56; berries, 93, 95, 96; hunting, 95. *See also* Iyall, Bill; Lahalet; Leschi; Muck-a-Muck; Owhi; Reed-Squally, Karen; Saluskin; Sluiskin; Wapowety (Opowety)
Naturalists, x. *See also* Schmoe, Floyd
Nelson, Lee, 10
News Tribune (Tacoma), 10–11, 83
Nisqually Glacier, 21–22, 23, 24, 52; and bridge, 16; and flood, 17; and road, 75
Northern Pacific Railroad, 20, 47, 51; and Carbon Glacier, 24; and Yellowstone, 57; and Mount Rainier National Park, 58, 59, 69; and hotels, 78

Oakes, T. F., 20
O'Farrell, Thomas, 91, 102–3
Ohanapecosh, 52, 101–2
Orting: and mudflows, 16
Osceola Mudflow, 13. *See also* Mudflows
Outburst floods, ix, 16–18. *See also* Mudflows
Overland Monthly, 50
Owhi, 88, 91

Paradise: weather, 16; snow, 24, 82, 83; visitors to, 34; meadow restoration, 35; camps at, 53, 89; and fire, 64–65; popularity of, 69; and cars, 75. *See also* Paradise Ice Caves; Paradise Inn; Skiing
Paradise Ice Caves, 24, 85
Paradise Inn: in winter, 27, 65, 66, 119–20; construction of, 78–79, 81; and ski troops, 111